ADOLF HANSEN and COLLEAGUES

BECOMING A DISCIPLE

a lifelong venture

experiences
follows
demonstrates
shares

yearns
anticipates
participates
serves

ABINGDON PRESS

NASHVILLE

BECOMING A DISCIPLE: A LIFELONG VENTURE

Copyright © 2015 by Adolf Hansen

All rights reserved.

Library of Congress Cataloging in Publication Data

ISBN 978-1-501-80504-2

15 16 17 18 19 20 21 22 23 24—10 9 8 7 6 5 4 3 2 1

MANUFACTURED IN THE UNITED STATES OF AMERICA

To

THOSE WHO ARE DISCIPLES OF JESUS CHRIST
at every point on the theological spectrum,
that we may understand, accept, and love one another,
in such a way that
THOSE GOD IS CALLING TO BE DISCIPLES OF JESUS CHRIST
may become disciples.

CONTENTS

Chapter 4

Chapter 5

Chapter 6

Chapter 7

Chapter 8

PART TWO: PROCESS
A disciple of Jesus Christ is a person who . . .

Chapter 9

Chapter 10

FOREWORD

"The mission of the Church is to make disciples of Jesus Christ for the transformation of the world." Those words, and that value, began appearing in our *Book of Discipline* when the 1996 General Conference approved a proposal from the delegation of the North Indiana Conference to add this statement under the section of the duties of the Annual Conference: "The purpose of the Annual Conference is to make disciples of Jesus Christ by equipping its local churches for ministry and by providing a connection for ministry beyond the local church; all to the glory of God" (¶601 in the 1996 *Discipline*). The South Indiana Conference delegation joined in supporting that proposal, along with many other conferences and groups, and the priority of "making disciples" began to permeate *The Book of Discipline* and our denomination.

I was elected a bishop of The United Methodist Church in July of 1996 by the North Central Jurisdiction, so I have had the privilege of watching this whole movement toward clarifying and emphasizing our mission/purpose as a United Methodist Church. Subsequent General Conferences have placed similar language throughout *The Book of Discipline*, including an addition proposed by the Council of Bishops in 2004 to add the phrase "for the transformation of the world" as a way of indicating the "so that" of our mission statement. We help people become disciples of Jesus so that we may participate in the transformation of the world that God is already accomplishing. Today the statement has received widespread support and affirmation. Almost every annual conference uses that mission statement; most local congregations use the mission statement and then add their own "vision statement" of how they are called to share in the mission in their unique setting. In fact, the vast majority of United Methodist people I meet in Indiana and throughout the world can quote our mission statement. From a historical and institutional perspective, that has all happened in fewer than twenty years, which is an amazing, monumental change of our denomination—bringing us more into alignment with our Wesleyan values and energizing our church to be in ministry and mission.

Since we are a diverse denomination, people emphasize this mission statement somewhat differently. For some, the first words are most important, and they emphasize bringing people to Christ through proclamation and evangelism. Others emphasize the latter part of the statement, and they focus upon social justice, missions, and witness. Some only see our mission statement from the institutional perspective of increasing our membership, while many others see the statement as a directive regarding participation in the kingdom of God.

This book is an effort to continue the conversation that began with a proposal from United Methodist clergy and laity in Indiana. When I was assigned in 2004 to come back to Indiana and lead the two conferences as they considered merging into one conference, great energy arose around the idea of creating a new conference, starting with "a blank sheet of paper." We called the process "Imagine Indiana" from the great prayer in Ephesians 3:20-21, which asks for the church to be blessed by God who is able "to accomplish abundantly far more than all we can ask or imagine" (NRSV). During the years 2004–2008, hundreds of clergy and laity were involved in helping to imagine and create a new Indiana Conference, and in 2008 both conferences gave an approval vote in excess of 75 percent to launch the new conference.

As the "Imagine Indiana" process developed, it became clear to us that *The Book of Discipline* does not provide either a definition of the word *disciple* or a clear description of the process for "becoming a disciple." A team led by Adolf Hansen, a retired seminary professor and Theologian in Residence at Indianapolis's St. Luke's UMC, developed a definition of *disciple*, which was approved by the new Indiana Conference and which is the basis of this book. In preparation for this action, I shared this definition in face-to-face meetings in all eighteen districts of the North and South Indiana Conferences. The response was not only positive but also enthusiastic!

I am very pleased that we have eight younger and newer clergy who have written chapters that will provide insights about the process of becoming a disciple. I have enjoyed their rich and vital conversations in preparation for this book.

What began in Indiana with a proposal to clarify the mission/purpose of our United Methodist Church now continues with an invitation for our readers to deepen the conversation around the meaning of discipleship and the lifelong process of becoming the disciples of Jesus we are called to be. The movement continues. Our UMC is moving forward in many important ways. Clarity of purpose and direction helps us find our way. Joining God in the transformation of the world is an amazing goal. It is the prayer of our writing team that this book can add to the movement. May it be so, Lord, may it be so.

Michael J. Coyner
Bishop, Indiana Conference
The United Methodist Church

PREFACE

Becoming a Disciple of Jesus Christ in the Twenty-first Century

It may sound like an easy venture, but it's not. Jesus himself set forth the conditions: "If any want to become my followers, let them deny themselves and take up their cross and follow me" (Mark 8:34 NRSV).

How can we understand what this means? How can we express that meaning in a way that will make a difference in our lives? How can we embody it in a way that will transform the world?

In an attempt to answer these questions, eight clergy—ordained as elders in the years 2008 through 2013—have each written a chapter in the book. Four of them went directly from college to seminary. Four entered a profession after completing college (business, education, law), before going to seminary. They attended five different institutions: Asbury Theological Seminary, Candler School of Theology, Christian Theological Seminary,

Duke Divinity School, and Garrett-Evangelical Theological Seminary. They currently serve in a variety of ministries and locations (identified on pages 156–57 at the end of the book).

Another elder with a career in higher education has written additional chapters that describe numerous ways individuals begin the process of becoming disciples of Jesus Christ, and subsequently move ahead at differing paces and in varying directions.

These writers currently serve in Indiana, though one or more of them previously lived in ten other states (California, Colorado, Georgia, Illinois, Kansas, Kentucky, Missouri, New York, North Carolina, Tennessee) and two other countries (England and Haiti). Furthermore, one or more spent time in fifty-one additional countries as well as all seven continents. Therefore, their perspective and understanding come from a wide geographical and cultural awareness of the church and the world.

Stories that grow out of the lives of the authors, together with those that emerge from the lives of others in varied places of ministry, permeate the book. In some instances names and selective details regarding individuals have been changed to protect their identities.

The authors of this book are grateful for the two episcopal leaders who have contributed to this volume. Michael Coyner, bishop of the Indiana Area of The UMC, has written the foreword. In addition, he is the bishop under whose appointment all of the writers serve.

Bruce Ough, bishop of the Dakotas-Minnesota Area of The UMC, has written the afterword. He is also the chairperson of the Connectional Table, a leadership group that serves as the visioning body of The United Methodist Church and the steward of resources to carry out that vision around the world.

A number of other individuals have made significant

contributions to this project. Family members and close friends of the authors have offered comments and suggestions, as well as a great deal of encouragement. Holly Miller, writing coach, has enhanced the exposition by her mastery of language and its meaningful expression.

Introducing the Venture

Adolf Hansen

As Jesus was walking beside the Sea of Galilee, he saw two brothers, Simon called Peter and his brother Andrew. They were casting a net into the lake, for they were fisherman. "Come, follow me," Jesus said. (Matthew 4:18-19)

One morning I turned on my iPhone, clicked on the Facebook app, and immediately saw a colorful image someone had sent me during the night. It was the earthly Jesus, clothed in a lengthy garment, sitting outdoors on a bench, his head turned toward a young man, and saying: "No, I'm not talking about Twitter. I literally want you to follow me."

In our social media world we frequently talk about "following." In Twitter, for example, we receive tweets from those we follow, and send tweets to those who follow us. However, it's rather uncommon to connect "following" with the invitation Jesus gave, first to Peter and Andrew, then James and John, and then the rest of the disciples—the invitation he also extends to us today.

The word *follow* is common in the New Testament (NRSV), showing up a total of 133 times, 90 of which are in the Gospels. Its root meaning is "to come after." However, in its broader context, it includes such delineations as moving in the same direction, accepting guidance, learning, putting into practice, and giving allegiance.

Furthermore, followers are often called *disciples*. Yet this word, whether singular or plural, is used in only five books in the New Testament: Matthew, Mark, Luke, John, and the Acts of the Apostles. It appears frequently in those books—240 times in the Gospels, and 30 in Acts. However, it is not used in any of the other 22 books in the New Testament, or the other 39 books of the Old Testament.

In other contexts the word *disciple* is also prevalent. A person can be a disciple of a figure in the past—John Wesley, Lucy Rider Meyer, Martin Luther King, Jr., or Mother Teresa. Or, a person in the present—Desmond Tutu, Rachel Held Evans, Billy Graham, or Pope Francis. Or, a disciple of a musician, an athlete, a politician, a renowned thinker, or a leader in another faith.

In the New Testament there were disciples of John the Baptist (Matthew 9:14), the Pharisees (Matthew 22:15-16), and a variety of other individuals and groups such as those named by Paul (1 Corinthians 1:12). Most significant, however, were those who became disciples of Jesus Christ—those who first experienced him as their earthly teacher and later as their risen Lord. These experiences led the disciples to become witnesses to Jesus' life, death, and resurrection in locations close to where they lived and then to areas throughout the Mediterranean world.

As time went on, the disciples incorporated into their lives what they had learned from Jesus when he said that those who wanted to be his followers had to deny themselves, take up their cross, and follow him (Matthew 16:24; Mark 8:34; Luke 9:23). This meant they had to do more than learn his teachings. They had to develop a relationship with him that would result in a life permeated with the presence of their risen Lord.

It is with this understanding that we have written this book. It is rooted in the New Testament understanding of Jesus Christ as a human being and a resurrected Lord. At the same time, this book is rooted in the concept of *becoming*—a compound of *be* and *come*. This word was popularized by Gordon Allport when he published a book with the title *Becoming* and the subtitle *Basic Considerations for a Psychology of Personality*.[1] It is a word used in many contexts, whether it refers to something positive, negative, or without any value judgment at all.

As noted in the foreword, the titles of the first eight chapters replicate the definition of the word *disciple* that was adopted by the Indiana Conference in 2009, the year the North Indiana Conference and the South Indiana Conference became a new conference. This definition has eight distinct components that give us the titles of the first eight chapters of this book.

Each of these chapters implicitly begins with the words "A disciple of Jesus Christ," followed by a verb in the present tense: (1) experiences, (2) follows, (3) demonstrates, (4) shares, (5) serves, (6) participates, (7) anticipates, and (8) yearns. The reason for using this tense is that it sets forth a continuous action. This means each verb is describing an ongoing experience, not a one-time event.

Furthermore, these statements are not set forth in an experiential order, since individuals can become engaged at different points in the process. Instead, they are organized in a logical manner. The first one refers to God, the second to Jesus Christ, and the third to the Holy Spirit. The next three refer to practices within a community of disciples. The seventh has a future perspective, both in this life and the life to come. The eighth is an outgrowth of the first seven in that it looks to the formation of other disciples.

Following the chapters that define what a disciple is, three additional chapters analyze varying processes individuals may go through. And, like the preceding chapters, each of them begins with a verb in the present tense. Chapter 9 identifies where a person may begin the process of becoming a disciple of Jesus Christ—at any one of the first seven possibilities. Chapter 10 explores where a person may move next—to any of the other possibilities. Chapter 11 examines other factors that may impact one's discipleship venture.

The twelfth and final chapter exemplifies the subtitle of the book, *A Lifelong Venture*. The present tense of the verbs that begin each of the first eleven chapters already imply that discipleship is a journey throughout life. It thereby never ends, at least in this life, unless a person chooses to no longer continue on this path. Furthermore, a journey that includes a degree of uncertainty regarding outcomes and incorporates some element of risk is more accurately known as a "venture." For this reason the subtitle affirms that the process of becoming a disciple may move along a path that, at times, meanders through unfamiliar or even unknown territory.

A brief section dealing with next steps that might be taken in the venture concludes the book. It encourages readers to reflect on the chapters they have read and to discern ways to use what they have learned. Hopefully, this book will make a difference in the lives of individuals or groups such as congregations, districts, or conferences in The United Methodist Church, as well as groups within other judicatories that carry out their ministry as disciples of Jesus Christ.

Becoming a Disciple correlates in a very direct manner with the mission of The United Methodist Church as stated in *The Book of Discipline* (¶120): "To make disciples of Jesus Christ for the transformation of the world," though the verb "make" in that statement sometimes lacks clarity and creates confusion. In the original language of Matthew 28:19—the verse in which Jesus says "Go and make disciples of all nations"—the verb *matheteuo* simply means "to disciple." The word *make* is not in the Greek text. To complicate the matter further, some church leaders talk about *discipling* people after they have become disciples, rather than recognizing that discipling incorporates the entire process.

The mission statement also contains a second sentence that must not be forgotten when speaking of the mission of The United Methodist Church: "Local churches provide the most significant arena through which disciple-making occurs." And that is not all! Local churches also provide powerful channels through which the transformation of the world takes place.

The overall statement of the mission has been embraced by many annual conferences across the nation and around the world. Therefore, the use of this book beyond the Indiana Conference is not only possible but also likely, as a means of encouragement toward deepening dialogue and mutual learning. In addition, the support given the overall mission by various theological perspectives within The United Methodist Church may bring groups such as the Good News Movement and the Confessing Movement on the one hand, and the Methodist Federation for Social Action and the Reconciling Ministries Network on the other, closer together. For there is considerable common ground in the way this book clarifies what it means to be a disciple (chapters 1–8) and how persons can become disciples (chapters 9–12).

Whatever impact the book will have in the life of the church will be up to the ones who read it, and the One who speaks through it—all to the glory of God!

1. Gordon Allport, *Becoming: Basic Considerations for a Psychology of Personality*, (New Haven: Yale University Press, 1960).

PART ONE: DEFINITION

A disciple of Jesus Christ is a person who...

CHAPTER 1

Experiences the Forgiveness and Acceptance of God

Brent Wright

Jesus said, "I am the light of the world. Whoever follows me won't walk in darkness but will have the light of life." (John 8:12)

I had dreaded this moment for a long time. I had avoided it as long as I could. Awful stereotypes about the people I might encounter swirled in my head, labels like *weirdo* and *sicko, creep,* and *loser.* I was scared I'd see someone I knew. I found what I thought was the right room in the unfamiliar church's basement, took a deep breath, and walked through the door into the small space. Was this the right meeting? I wasn't about to ask anyone, since that might require naming the meeting I was looking for. So I sat down at the table with the other five people, trying to look nonchalant, unable to make eye contact with anyone, wanting to be anywhere but there. I would have given anything to be invisible.

The meeting began when someone said, with surprising cheer, "Hi, I'm Bob, I'm a sex addict, and I'll be serving as the chairperson today." I felt a mixture of relief and shame.

I was in the right meeting.

SECRET WORLD

Even though the walk from my car to that room only took a few minutes, I had been headed for that meeting for years. I don't know when my sexuality mutated from that of a normal adolescent to that of an addict, but I had been abusing pornography for a long time. I was a good church boy, a careful rule-follower in public. But I had a secret world when I was alone. Over the years, the pathways of sexual stimulation in my brain and my body had become my drug, my go-to mechanism for coping with life. Porn drew me away from people into a private fantasy world, and in that place, I didn't have to act. My life had become an elaborate play of sorts, and I was starring as the person I thought I was supposed to be. I played the role of my public self by day and hid alone in my cave at night. I was a gregarious person in public, busy and involved, known by many; but no one knew the whole me. The fake relationships peddled by porn were my sad substitute for real connection. And that counterfeit experience had me in its grip just like any other addictive substance; I had tried repeatedly to fix my problem on my own, but it only grew worse. I was a slave to this well-hidden evil in me, and I was profoundly alone, even during the time I was part of an intimate seminary community.

LONGING FOR INTIMACY

That's the essence of sin: separation from what's most real and true. My sin separated me from *others*, as I withdrew and as the unreal world of porn distorted my perception. My sin separated me from *God*, as shame drove me to hide just like Adam and Eve with their fig leaves. My sin even separated me from my *self*, as I lost the ability to be real, to be open and honest, even in the privacy of my own thoughts. I was living my version of the Apostle Paul's confession: "I don't know what I'm doing, because I don't do what

4

I want to do. Instead, I do the thing that I hate" (Romans 7:15).

Intimacy is our most basic hunger as creatures made in the image of the triune God. Our souls yearn for closeness from our first day of life, through belonging to clubs or teams as children, through awkward adolescent attempts at connection and love, through working to build deep attachment in lifelong partnership, through the season of loss at the end of life.

Sin is whatever wedges its way in and tears apart, working against our God-given gravity toward intimacy. Sin often appears on the surface as bad behavior of one sort or another, but those behaviors are only the tip of the iceberg. Most of sin is below the surface. Whatever the behaviors, sin is separation.

Forgiveness, then, is the opposite: forgiveness is restoring intimacy. Forgiveness is when God removes the wedge of sin that broke the connection between me and God, between me and others, between me and my very self. Forgiveness is reconnection. Embrace God's voice affirming, "You are my child and I love you no matter what."

ADMITTING THE TRUTH TO MYSELF

"Hi, I'm Bob, I'm a sex addict, and I'll be serving as the chairperson today."

"Hi, Bob," everyone replied.

Bob continued, reading the script in front of him. "This is a closed meeting for sex addicts and persons desiring their own sexual sobriety..." Blah, blah, blah. I could barely pay attention. My mind was flooded with thoughts of the journey that had brought me to this place, even while I tried to accept that I was here, at an actual twelve-step meeting, with real addicts.

I had been resisting this step for a long time because I was afraid. On the surface, I was afraid of exposure. I was serving as an associate pastor at a large suburban church, and thousands of people knew my face. What if one of them saw me going into a meeting? Below the surface, I was afraid of admitting to myself that I couldn't stop this self-destructive behavior. I was afraid that I was defective and unlovable.

As much as I wanted to be free of the addiction, those fears had stopped me from getting help for several years. By God's grace, I had slowly begun to confess the truth, first to a seminary friend, and then to the psychologist evaluating my psych testing as part of the ordination candidacy process. Even after she referred me to twelve-step recovery, I was still paralyzed by fear for three more years. Only when the Board of Ordained Ministry made it clear that recovery was mandatory did I finally get the help I needed. I found a twelve-step meeting in a non–United Methodist church on my day off, and I forced myself through the door.

"If this is your first time attending this fellowship, please introduce yourself by your first name." My face flushed. That's me. It felt like I was stepping off a cliff when I said, for the first time, "Hi. I'm Brent, and I'm a sex addict." It didn't feel real, but I was pretty sure it was true. It didn't matter to the others around the table; they simply said, "Hi, Brent. Welcome."

And then they applauded.

More than nine years later, that memory still brings tears to my eyes. I've been to meetings nearly every week since then and there's no way to count how many times I've introduced myself as a sex addict in meetings. But I'm still amazed by the embrace of that moment when the group applauded the first time I spoke that truth out loud. That embrace changed my life. That embrace began to remove the shackles of shame that had handicapped my ability to connect with others. That embrace was God.

I am an addict: those four words took years to work their way into my consciousness and come out of my mouth. Speaking them aloud—the beginning of a journey called recovery—was a milestone on my lifelong journey as a disciple of Jesus Christ.

TELLING THE TRUTH FACE-TO-FACE

The spiritual sense of embrace I felt in that first meeting follows honesty, and the more vulnerable the truth-telling, the more significant the embrace. When people are open and real, whatever it is they're sharing, connection is the result. This is most obvious when a person begins to cry; a tender opening happens in others who are present. Tears are raw emotion, a completely real expression of what's overflowing from our hearts. When tears begin to flow, hearts swell and embrace happens, if not physically, then emotionally. That embrace, that compassion, is divine.

We are forgiven and accepted—by others and by God—as a response to telling the whole truth as best we're able. While it is possible for this to happen in the privacy of our hearts, telling the truth to another human being is a much richer experience. Twelve-step communities follow in the footsteps of the church through history in taking seriously the New Testament letter's instruction to "confess your sins to one another, and pray for one another, so that you may be healed" (James 5:16 NRSV). Note that James specifically encouraged confession *to one another*, not just to God. I imagine this is because he knew that connecting with others *is* connecting with God. Being real with another person leaves us with a peace that is remarkably like what we feel when we are real with God. Connecting to God and others are intertwined experiences.

Telling the truth about secrets is freeing. When Jesus proclaims, "I am the light of the world. Whoever follows me won't walk in darkness" (John 8:12), I hear an invitation to open our souls to the light. It's as if Jesus is saying, *You don't have to hide that ugly stuff or pretend it's not there. Swing the closet door wide open so the light can reach all the way to that dark corner.* "If you continue in my word, you are truly my disciples; and you will know the truth, and the truth will make you free" (John 8:31-32 NRSV). Free from what? *Free from your slavery to sin,* he clarifies a few verses later. Knowing the truth—not just about Jesus, but about myself, too—results in freedom.

Telling the truth about secrets is frightening. The closer I get to the stuff that's hidden in the back corner of the closet, the more every fiber of my being resists letting in the light. That's shame triggering my fear. Trying to experience intimacy while driven by fear and shame is like trying to hug someone while wearing a suit of armor. Shame is the armor that gets in the way of experiencing the full embrace of God or others.

Telling the truth to another human being opens a door between us. It encourages others to know and tell their own truth in response, connecting us. It creates reconnection with self, as the denial that disconnected me from the reality of my self melts away. It reconnects us to God, allowing God to reach right to where the wedge of sin tore us apart and bring forgiveness.

PERFECTIONISM IN THE CHURCH

The culture of church most of us know, rather than freeing us, reinforces fear and shame and makes it harder to connect with one another or with God. Part of this culture comes from a misunderstanding of one of Jesus' best-known commands in the Sermon on the Mount: "Be perfect, therefore, as your heavenly Father is perfect" (Matthew 5:48 NRSV). In the age of machines and microscopes, perfection has come to mean "without fault"; so Jesus' command often sounds like it means "eliminate errors."

Holiness gets equated with flawlessness and that damages church culture. Alongside this understanding of perfection, many see God as an uncompromising cosmic scorekeeper, punishing every bad thought or deed with a demerit, and many believe the afterlife means eternal torment for those persons with unforgiven demerits on their cards. In this frame (even softened versions of it), the stakes are enormous if a person commits sin. Rather than encouraging honesty, high stakes do the opposite, and many of us live in denial of the reality inside our soul's closet. This common merciless theological paradigm works against honesty and openness with God and with one another.

We see this in the culture of many churches. For many committed disciples of Jesus, church is the *last* place they would tell the truth about their brokenness. Twentieth-century pastor and theologian Dietrich Bonhoeffer said in *Life Together* that our habit of only sharing the devout parts of our lives with fellow church members means church becomes a place for pious people, not sinners, and many Christians react with horror when they discover the sin of a church member. The result: church becomes a dishonest community where sin is denied and concealed, rather than named and forgiven. The Pharisees' error of self-righteous hypocrisy is still standard fare in churches, despite the best intentions of most disciples of Jesus.

Within the body of Christ, the community characterized by grace and love, we're rarely real with one another. We hide the truth of our sin from everyone around us and often from ourselves. And that is the same as hiding it from God, even if we've tried to confess in the privacy of our prayers. How we are with others is how we are with God, so when we're not willing to be open and honest with our neighbors, we're not being open and honest with God. Like Adam and Eve, we're tying on fig leaves, covering the parts of ourselves of which we are ashamed.

9

EXPOSED AND EMBRACED

The first step in twelve-step addiction recovery is: *We admitted we were powerless over our addiction—that our lives had become unmanageable.* Often, recovering addicts will take this step by sharing the story of their addiction in a meeting. After a couple of years in recovery, the time had come to share my story.

In the two years that had gone by since my first twelve-step meeting, I had been appointed to a different congregation about forty-five minutes away from my first church. After the move, I had begun to attend one of the healthiest meetings in the city—a group that met in my previous church. The room where the meeting was held was fifty feet from my former office. For several years, I had worked in this building as a well-known spiritual leader. Now I came to this place for recovery.

I hadn't planned it this way, but when the time came that I knew I was ready to take a next step in my recovery by sharing my story out loud in a meeting, the opportunity landed on the darkest day of the Christian year. I began that Good Friday in the cold, predawn dark, driving to the place I had served as pastor to name my most personal pain and brokenness in community. At the end of the day, I would put on my robe and stole and lead my own congregation in worship. But first, I opened myself to God by taking a vulnerable step in my own discipleship.

I talked about what behaviors are addictive for me, how the addiction had progressed over time, and my failed attempts to stop. I felt lonely despite being with twenty other people. I was ashamed and afraid of their judgment. I felt like I was disfigured and was carefully displaying my disfigurement to others. I hated this part of myself. I wanted to run away and hide.

While I talked, when I had the courage to look at the others around the room, I saw looks of compassion and recognition. I saw some tears roll down cheeks. I didn't see pity or judgment. When I finished, the group simply applauded. I felt both relief and fear; while my sharing was finished, now they would offer feedback. One by one, my friends and acquaintances chimed in with gratitude and connection. It didn't have anything at all to do with the quality of my presentation or the specifics of my shame. Even when their stories were different from mine, they found points of connection and spoke them out loud. My loneliness had melted away. I felt sad for the reality of the story I had spoken, but at the same time, I felt gratitude for the spiritual intimacy it had opened up. I felt embraced, not just by my fellow addicts, but by God.

I was experiencing the restoration of intimacy that is the heart of God's forgiveness. Perhaps it was this exposure and embrace that inspired the psalmist to begin a song with, "LORD, you have examined me. You know me" (Psalm 139:1). This intimacy comes from integrity with self, where there's no more division between the public me and the private me, between the part of me I acknowledge and the part of me I deny. Serenity comes from being fully exposed and being embraced in response. That's divine love.

BIBLICAL PERFECTION

My journey of recovery and discipleship didn't end on that Good Friday, of course—that was step one of twelve, and after working through them multiple times, those steps have become a way of life. My experience of intimacy with God and others through truth-telling in recovery is changing me as a husband, father, friend, and preacher. Once I tasted freedom from having to hide my addiction, I wanted to learn how to be honest in everything. I wanted to learn how to *be real*. This is truth-telling that goes beyond sharing facts about myself to taking the risk of being open about what I feel and think and want. It means being fully present; rather than morphing into what I think people want me to be, I aim to be most fully myself.

This is what Jesus was talking about when he said, "Be perfect." The Greek word translated "perfect" in many translations doesn't mean *flawless*. It means *complete* or *whole* or *mature*, as in the Common English Bible translation of Matthew 5:48: "Therefore, just as your heavenly Father is complete in showing love to everyone, so also you must be complete." I've learned that a whole human being isn't one without error or brokenness. A complete human is one who is real, who is honest about what's true inside. To be otherwise is like the foot saying it's unworthy because it's not a hand, to use Paul's analogy (1 Corinthians 12). The Creator is honored by creatures who are most fully themselves, most completely as they are. "Be perfect" isn't about overcoming our humanness; it's about being fully human.

Just as living in a culture of perfectionism leaves no room for truth-telling (as many of us experience in church), the opposite is also true. When one person has the faith and courage to be real, it encourages others to be real. When some people are willing to be their whole flawed selves, there's room in the community for others to grow in that direction. Vulnerability encourages gentleness. Openness engenders connection, which generates compassion and intimacy. Honesty is contagious.

WORK IN PROGRESS

Today I am experiencing Jesus' promise that "the truth will set you free." I am free to be real about imperfection and to keep growing. I'm free to keep confessing and receiving God's forgiveness and acceptance.

When I walked into that first meeting, I thought, *How long will*

I have to do this? I just wanted to stop looking at porn and get on with my life. I'd do what I needed to, but it was a real headache having to go to meetings and do all the work necessary for the twelve steps. I had once thought that way about being a Christian: what do I have to do to get my Get-Into-Heaven card punched?

Today I understand the grace-filled truth: I get to be an addict in ongoing recovery, just like I get to be a disciple of Jesus Christ in ongoing spiritual growth. Recovery no longer revolves around avoiding bad behavior, just like discipleship no longer revolves around getting into heaven. I'm no longer a slave to porn as my coping mechanism, and I'm no longer devoting all my spiritual energy to avoiding sins. Along the way, I began to understand that both recovery and discipleship are about far more than stopping destructive behavior. They're about learning how to live the life of openness and connection that God intends for all God's children. They're not only about receiving freedom *from* addiction or sin, they're about receiving freedom *for* abundant life in relationship with God and others.

While *my* story of experiencing God's forgiveness and acceptance is grounded in recovery, the twelve-step community is only one tool that God is using to embrace the broken. God is at work reconnecting what sin has torn apart in every community, large and small, formal and informal, religious and not.

Occasionally these days, I take my turn as the one who begins the meeting with "Hi, I'm Brent, I'm a sex addict, and I'll be serving as the chairperson today."

I usually feel a mixture of gratitude and love for the people gathered around the table in another church basement.

I am in the right meeting.

QUESTIONS

1. Have you experienced the forgiveness and acceptance of God? If so, think of a time when that was true. If not, why do you think you haven't?

2. Think of a time when you felt fully seen, embraced, accepted. How did that happen? Was the setting a "sacred" one? As you look back on it, how do you see God in it?

3. What thought or behavior leaves you feeling most alone? Who could you imagine sharing this with? What might you feel if you did? Imagine that when you tell them, they respond, "Me, too!" What might that feel like?

4. Has anyone ever confessed to you? What did it feel like? What was your heart's response? Did you find yourself telling the truth about yourself in response?

5. Think of a time when someone you love deeply cried in your presence. What did that feel like?

RESOURCES

Breathing Under Water: Spirituality and the Twelve Steps, by Richard Rohr. Cincinnati, OH: St. Anthony Messenger Press, 2011.

Life Together: A Discussion of Christian Fellowship, by Dietrich Bonhoeffer. New York: Harper & Row, 1954.

I Thought It Was Just Me (But It Isn't): Making the Journey from "What Will People Think?" to "I Am Enough," by Brené Brown. New York: Gotham, 2007.

Learning to Walk in the Dark, by Barbara Brown Taylor. New York: HarperCollins, 2014.

Pastrix: The Cranky, Beautiful Faith of a Sinner & Saint, by Nadia Bolz-Weber. Nashville: Jericho Books, 2013.

Intimacy, by Henry J. M. Nouwen. New York: HarperCollins, 1969.

Resident Aliens: Life in the Christian Colony, by Stanley Hauerwas & William H. Willimon. Nashville: Abingdon Press, 1989.

The Prodigal God: Recovering the Heart of the Christian Faith, by Timothy Keller. New York: Penguin Group, 2008.

CHAPTER 2

Follows the Life and Teachings of Jesus Christ

Jill Moffett Howard

Jesus said..., "I am the way, the truth, and the life." (John 14:6)

"You don't believe in Jesus? Then you're going to hell!" I heard these words often as a Jewish teenager growing up in the Bible Belt of East Tennessee. I always thought Christians would have a hard time getting people to follow Jesus if the only way to make that happen was to scare them. As a Jewish youth, I didn't know much about Jesus. I knew he was a Jew, some called him Rabbi, and he was a caring, compassionate teacher. My Jewish faith and tradition taught me that much. It also taught me he was not divine, he was not the Son of God or the Messiah, and he definitely was not a popular topic of conversation in Hebrew school. But as I once heard author Anne Lamott say, "The Holy Spirit very rarely respects one's comfort zones." I found this to be true as God gradually opened my heart to the life and teachings of Jesus during my senior year of high school through a class called Bible History.

This was not a religious class, but a chance to explore the many facets of the Bible, its stories, and its people. My eyes were opened to the real Jesus who did not send people to hell, but healed the sick, loved the unlovable, and challenged his followers to see the world in new ways. I finally began to see the real Jesus as loving, compassionate, and inclusive; not hateful, judgmental, and exclusive. I had to know more. So I began to study, ask questions, and block out all the "noise" that distracted me from discovering the real Jesus. I eventually went to church and got involved in a youth group, but I still had a lot of questions. I struggled mainly with these questions: Who is Jesus? Is he just a man? A good teacher? Someone who worked miracles? Or is he divine? The Son of God? The Messiah? God in human form?

ASKING THE CENTRAL QUESTION

My studies of the Gospels of Matthew, Mark, and Luke eventually led me to the question that Jesus asks his disciples, "Who do the crowds say that I am?" After receiving some vague answers, Jesus asks them again, directly this time, "And what about you? Who do *you* say that I am?" (Luke 9:18, 20, emphasis added). I realized that my faith journey, and arguably all Christian faith journeys, should begin by wrestling with this one question from Jesus. Perhaps this is the central question of the Christian faith: "Who do you say that I am?" Peter's response in each Gospel is the same: "You are the Christ." My hope was to get to the bottom of the meaning of his answer and to claim it for my own. What would it mean for me to claim Jesus as the Christ? My answering this question took me deep into the heart of my faith. It required study, scripture, and wrestling with myself at my very core. I knew that professing Jesus as the Christ would change my life in ways I was not ready to accept. It would challenge my faith in ways for which I was not prepared. It was a choice I was not sure I was ready to make. Eventually, after almost giving up, I was able to open my mind to the possibilities and address Jesus' question, "Who do you say I am?" I was able to respond: "You are the Christ."

The journey of faith begins for all of us with our answer to this question. We say, "You are the Christ." We might say it boldly, or we might say it with a shaking voice, with questions or doubts still stirring in our hearts, not knowing what lies ahead. That is certainly where I found myself. But I believe that his acceptance of our profession, regardless of how we profess it, is still the same. He says to us, "I am the way, the truth, and the life," and then he extends the invitation of a lifetime: "Follow me."

When Jesus calls us to follow him, he invites us on a lifelong journey to come alongside him, to walk with him and be challenged by him. Interestingly, the Greek word that is most often translated for *follow* is rooted in the word for *road*. To follow Jesus is to share the same road. Jesus invites us not to be complacent followers, but to be followers who actively seek ways to imitate his life and teachings and live them out in the world. To follow Jesus is to adopt the Christlike attitude of humility, putting the interests of others before our own and loving our neighbors as we love ourselves. May we venture to be like Thomas in the Gospel of John when he says to Jesus, "Lord, we don't know where you are going. How can we know the way?" and live our lives as a response to the Lord's answer: "I am the way, the truth, and the life" (John 14:5-6). To follow the life and teachings of Jesus Christ, we must seek him and follow him as such.

Following Jesus as the Way

As with every journey, the Way often begins with one step, one person, or one idea. As an example: Jamie is a young woman from a small town in Texas who attends a church primarily made up of older people of Caucasian ethnicity. The surrounding community, however, has a large Hispanic population. Jamie lives in town and works in the grocery store. She began to notice several young Hispanic women who were pregnant and didn't appear to have family support. After a time of discernment and praying for courage and guidance, Jamie reached out to some of these young women and discovered their need for safe space and a supportive community. Jamie approached the pastor of the church and several leaders, who agreed that Jamie could use space in the church building to launch a support group for the young women.

At first, some of the older members of the church opposed the idea, and Jamie became frustrated and saddened by their comments and resistance, but she was determined to press on. The meetings attracted only one or two women, but over time, the support group ministry grew to twenty-five or thirty women, some of whom started to attend the church regularly. The congregation's demographics gradually changed as Hispanic women and their children began to call the church their home. It was a place that welcomed and accepted them. It was a place where they experienced the amazing grace of God through Jesus Christ. They found the kingdom here on earth, thanks to one young woman who was willing to reach out and grasp the idea of the kingdom of God, and others along the way who helped build it. That is the Way of following Jesus.

A disciple of Jesus Christ is a person who follows the Way of Jesus. It is not one correct path, and there is no right or wrong way to begin the journey. The Way is a journey in itself during which we continue to explore how to live out our beliefs on a daily basis. We each have our own path along the Way, guided by our faith and the Holy Spirit. The Synoptic Gospels—Matthew, Mark, and Luke—give us indications of what the Way of Jesus looks like. These Gospels are primarily concerned with telling the story of

20

Jesus: his life, teachings, and ministry. The kingdom of heaven, or kingdom of God, is a primary focus. Jesus teaches his disciples what the kingdom of heaven is like and how we might experience the kingdom here and now. As he says in Luke's Gospel: "Don't you see? God's kingdom is already among you" (Luke 17:21). Jesus challenges his disciples as he challenges us today to accept that the kingdom is within our grasp if only we are willing to see it, work toward it, and build it together. The Way of Jesus consists of building the kingdom here and now, that we might begin to transform the world in his name.

The Way is not always easy, nor is it supposed to be. Disciples who follow the Way must be willing to accept the inevitable bumps and turns and know that they will not always succeed. Disciples who follow the Way must be bold and courageous, willing to face the hardships on the road ahead as they recall these words of Jesus: "All who want to come after me must say no to themselves, take up their cross daily, and follow me" (Luke 9:23). Jamie is an example of a person who was willing to experience the bumps and turns along the Way in order to follow Jesus and build the kingdom. She knew it would be a challenge and that some persons would refuse to accept her and the young women. She knew that the changes resulting from the new ministry would be hard for some, yet she was willing to take that first step in following Jesus, trusting in his guidance, and accepting his challenge. The Way of Jesus is one of humility and servanthood, as we are reminded that Jesus comes among us as one who serves. Disciples model this on the Way.

Following Jesus as the Truth

When I was that Jewish teenager years ago asking questions about Jesus, I desperately sought the truth. I wanted to know the truth about Jesus, who he was, and what, if anything, he revealed

21

about God. Most important at the time, I wanted to know what he meant for my life and faith. I experienced no "light bulb moment" when I accepted him as the Truth. He was revealed to me over time and in a variety of ways through people, experiences, moments of uncertainty and pain, and with the still, small voice of the Holy Spirit. I found that in my most vulnerable moments I began to experience Jesus as the Truth, and God was revealed to me in new ways. When I threw up my hands in frustration or sadness and said, "I just don't know! I believe; help my unbelief!" I felt the Truth revealed to me more clearly and was more willing to follow into the unknown.

Knowing the truth is very freeing, whether because we have known and seen what the non-truths are, or because we no longer are imprisoned by the lies of others or the lies we have been telling ourselves. When truth is spoken, power and courage come with it, even when we speak it with a shaking voice. What Jesus tells his followers may really be true: the truth will set you free.

I think it's safe to say that we all are seekers of truth. We might even find ourselves asking along with Pontius Pilate at the trial of Jesus: "What is truth?" (John 18:38). The most accurate translation of the Greek word for *truth* is "to come out of hiding, to be revealed, to be vulnerable, to portray a reality." In Jesus, God revealed the truth to all of humanity.

The beauty of the Christian story is that "truth" is a person, and that person is Jesus Christ. Truth is more than a statement or a concept. Truth, in this case, means a relationship between God and God's people. God reveals the Truth in Jesus Christ, who becomes vulnerable and humbled (even to death on a cross!) and comes out of hiding before us to reveal the love and grace of God to all of humanity. In the same way, Jesus invites us to experience him as the Truth, so that we may become vulnerable before God, humbling ourselves as we live out our daily lives.

Sometimes the truth is hard to hear or know for sure. It is challenging or makes us uncomfortable. Jesus is the Truth who challenges us to follow a different path. Throughout his ministry, Jesus confronts the people and harsh realities of his day and offers a better way. To follow the life and teachings of Jesus Christ means that we accept him as the Truth and are willing to confess along with Peter, "You are the Christ. You are the Truth." Then we are invited to accept the invitation of Jesus: "Follow me."

Confessing Jesus as the Truth does not mean we have to be perfect in words or actions. There is no right or wrong way to enter into the Truth that Jesus offers, no proper solution or prayer or "to do" list. He only asks for open hearts ready to receive him. In Paul's Letter to the Romans, we read, "If you confess with your mouth 'Jesus is Lord' and in your heart you have faith that God raised him from the dead, you will be saved. . . . All who call on the Lord's name will be saved" (Romans 10:9-13).

Throughout the Gospels we read stories of people coming to Jesus for healing. He doesn't ask them if they believe a certain way. He doesn't ask them to pray a certain prayer. He doesn't insist that they have the "correct" theology before they can be healed. He simply reaches out his hands or speaks the words and heals them. Oftentimes he says, "Your faith has healed you. Go in peace." We can also translate this as, "Your faith has saved you" or "Your faith has made you whole." When we see Jesus for who he is as the Truth, when we have faith that he can heal/save/make us whole, we are on our way to living a life of discipleship, a life of love and service. We are compelled to share the Truth with others. People are seeking the truth. People are seeking something different and challenging. People are seeking hope and peace. People are seeking the Truth. Where will they find it?

Following Jesus as the Life

Tia is a young woman whose parents were not involved in her life. She had few friends and had a history of abusive relationships with men. She was involved with drugs and alcohol. Feeling broken and alone, she began to cut her arms with razor blades several times a week and then several times a day. She felt she deserved the pain. Eventually, she cut herself so deeply that she ended up in the hospital where the hospital chaplain befriended her. He took an interest in her life and story. One day, the chaplain opened the Bible and read from the Gospel of Mark about Jesus healing the woman who had been bleeding for twelve years (Mark 5:25-34). Tia was especially struck by Jesus' response to the woman after he healed her: "Your faith has healed you; go in peace, healed from your disease" (verse 34). This story was the first step in Tia's journey toward wellness. She found comfort in knowing that Jesus saw this woman for who she was, loved her, had compassion on her, and sent her on her way as a healed and whole person. Tia recognized that Jesus had given the bleeding woman life, and he could do the same for her.

This is, after all, what Jesus came to do. He came so we might have life, and have it in abundance (John 10:10). In every healing story in the Gospels, we see Jesus speaking the words or reaching out his hands to heal. Then he sends the person into the world to live a new life to the fullest. Jesus, as the Life, gives life to those who seek him and wish to follow him. When we follow Jesus as the Life, we celebrate that we are to model our lives after an incarnate, life-giving deity who lived his whole life as a teaching. It is Jesus who came to live a messy human life with ordinary people, who died a human death, and who speaks life into places where there is fear, mistrust, and brokenness. When we follow Jesus as the Life, we also rejoice at his resurrection and victory over death, so that we may have life!

A disciple is a person who follows the life and teachings of Jesus because he is the Life and comes that we might model our lives after him. Oftentimes people do not feel worthy to be called disciples or Jesus followers because "discipleship" has been falsely described as living up to particular moral standards or following a strict set of rules in order to be a Christ follower. That is not what Jesus has in mind. We follow the life and teachings of Jesus so that we may be transformed not into perfect people, but into people who know that they are loved and accepted by a compassionate savior. Like Tia, we are compelled to follow Jesus as the Life because he is the giver of life, the healer of brokenness, the one who sends us forth to live our lives as whole persons. We follow Jesus as the Life because he has defeated sin and death.

Disciples are not persons who feel weighed down by the profession of faith that Jesus is Lord, but persons who long to share the joy that comes with following Jesus. When I was struggling to decide whether I wanted to be a part of the Christian journey, someone told me that I would have to give up certain things and had to behave in a certain way in order to follow Christ. Becoming a disciple is not meant to decrease your quality of life or ask you to follow a list of do's or don'ts. It is about seeing your life in a new way and surrendering it to the one who promises to give you abundant life. It is about reframing your old life so you may have new life modeled after Jesus Christ and lived out in service to God and others. When tentatively I took my first steps as a disciple of Jesus Christ, I walked as one ready to seek this abundant life. I was ready to seek life in the one who is the Life. When I look back now, I wonder what took me so long.

ANSWERING THE QUESTION

It all begins with a question from Jesus: "Who do you say that I am?" When we are ready to answer this question, we may find ourselves at a crossroads. Where to next? Which road should we choose? May we find that Jesus comes alongside us and says, "I am the Way, the Truth, and the Life. Follow me." Disciples of Jesus are challenged to follow and show others the Way, the Truth, and the Life. May we answer this question from Jesus with confidence, that we may find there is no better way to live, no more excellent path to follow, no other journey that is more life-giving than the journey of becoming a disciple.

QUESTIONS

1. *How do you answer Jesus' question: "Who do you say I am?"*

2. *How and when have you experienced Jesus as the Way? The Truth? The Life?*

3. *In what ways do you strive to follow the life and teachings of Jesus?*

4. *What challenges have you faced along the journey? How have you overcome them?*

5. *How will you invite others to follow the life and teachings of Jesus?*

RESOURCES

Evolving in Monkey Town: How a Girl Who Knew All the Answers Learned to Ask the Questions, by Rachel Held Evans. Grand Rapids, MI: Zondervan, 2010.

Following Jesus: Biblical Reflections on Discipleship, by N. T. Wright. Grand Rapids, MI: Eerdmans Publishing Company, 1995.

Following Jesus: Steps to a Passionate Faith, by Carolyn Slaughter. Nashville: Abingdon Press, 2008.

I Am a Follower: The Way, the Truth, and Life of Following Jesus, by Leonard Sweet. Nashville: Thomas Nelson, 2012.

Traveling Mercies: Some Thoughts on Faith, by Anne Lamott. New York: Anchor Books, 2000.

Velvet Elvis: Repainting the Christian Faith, by Rob Bell. New York: HarperOne, 2012.

To Write Love on Her Arms (www.twloha.com).

CHAPTER 3

Demonstrates the Fruit of the Spirit

Peter Curts

"The fruit of the Spirit is love, joy, peace, patience, kindness,
goodness, faithfulness, gentleness, and self-control."
(Galatians 5:22-23)

The call of a pastor is to make disciples of Jesus Christ for the transformation of the world. As a young seminarian I read books and took classes describing how the discipleship process unfolds. Then I arrived at my first pastoral assignment—three churches nestled in the hills of southern Indiana, each with a unique identity. I immediately felt the impact of the challenge that I faced. Leading persons to become disciples would compel me to speak to the very core of the congregations as I encouraged and shepherded each member's spiritual journey.

I remember sitting in my first parsonage talking to some clergy friends about my lack of confidence. "Who am I to think that I can spiritually lead these people?" I asked. "Many are more than twice my age!" The response from my friends and the message that God gave me that day was this: What I can offer is God at work in me. Making a difference is not rooted in my experience or brilliance. As my friends reminded me, the disciples of Jesus once argued this same question as they tried to figure out who among them was the greatest or who was doing the best job. Jesus replied, "Whoever wants to be first must be least of all and the servant of all" (Mark 9:35).

I wanted to be the best pastor I could be, but living in fear of failure would sabotage my best efforts. One slipup would remind me of my vulnerability. I know now that my calling is not to achieve perfection but to find perfection in the presence of God. The way of discipleship is the way of being fruitful. Discipleship is not measured by what we do. It is measured by the fruit that God grows in us.

SELFISH DESIRES

Before introducing the concept of fruit of the Spirit, Paul introduces us to another list. A common translation is the "works of the flesh." The Common English Bible translates the word *flesh* as a person's "selfish desires." To rely on the flesh is to rely on ourselves and not on God. We trust our own inclinations rather than rely on the Holy Spirit. The works of the flesh include "sexual immorality, moral corruption, doing whatever feels good, idolatry, drug use and casting spells, hate, fighting, obsession, losing your temper, competitive opposition, conflict, selfishness, group rivalry, jealousy, drunkenness, partying, and other things like that" (Galatians 5:19-21). What Paul is saying is that when we do not rely on the movement of God's Spirit, our souls tend to turn inward. On the one hand, we attempt to find satisfaction, but on the other, we end up feeling isolated and empty.

Works of the flesh are the result of living apart from the wisdom of God. For example, I remember my seventeenth birthday party, a time before I was a disciple of Jesus Christ. Tim and Steve arrived early, shortly after my mom had left the house to pick up the special cake she had ordered in my honor. Tim pulled out some pre-party beverages that were not age-appropriate and we took a drink, and then another. I still remember the sound of the door opening as my mom arrived home. I realized that we had made a big mistake, and I was deeply ashamed of myself. I had disappointed my mom, myself, and my God.

Years later, I understand my actions that day. My desire was to impress my friends in the best way that I knew how. On the surface, my activities were breaking the law. However, when I think about what was going on inside of me I realize that I was acting out of a deep loneliness. My choices were unwise, and were done out of a need to cover my wounds. I wanted to be accepted by others.

Since then I have found a new way to view myself and God. The Holy Spirit redefines the best *and* worst parts of me. Being a disciple means that I am still accepted by Christ. I live in the grace of God. My "worth" is measured by the fruit God produces in me.

Led by the Holy Spirit

The *fruit* of the Spirit is a singular word in the original Greek. This stands in contrast to the plural *works of the flesh*. Life in the flesh has many audiences to please. Do I like myself? Am I making my family happy? Am I doing a good enough job at work? On the other hand, living in the Spirit is simpler. Instead of being pulled in a variety of directions, we are led in one direction by the Holy Spirit. We begin with a foundation of being accepted and loved, and make our decisions out of that. We do not need to seek acceptance from anyone else.

Another implication is that the fruit go together. One fruit does not appear apart from the others. We are not meant to pick and choose from the fruit tree; we are called to exhibit all the fruit. This makes the fruit of the Spirit a high standard for living. Some days

I might do a good job at showing kindness to others. However, my self-control might be lacking.

Also, the fruit are qualities of character that are available to all persons. They are not dependent on personality or disposition. We may have one or two fruit that come easily because of our disposition. Nevertheless, it is difficult for any person to bear all the fruit at every moment. I know of some people who contribute a significant amount of time and energy to their community, yet they are harsh in style and cold in attitude. I know of others who make similar contributions, but do so in caring and loving ways. The list of fruit contains descriptors for how disciples are called to live.

Reliance on the Holy Spirit makes the fruit possible. Jesus gives us this image: "Abide in me as I abide in you. Just as the branch cannot bear fruit by itself unless it abides in the vine, neither can you unless you abide in me" (John 15:4 NRSV). There is an active and passive part to abiding. God encourages us to seek the Holy Spirit and to rely on God's understanding. The seeking of God is our active part. In the midst of finding God, we also rely on the Holy Spirit to empower our lives and our relationships. The passive part is our receptivity to God's voice in our inmost being. God wants to show light in all the places of brokenness and spiritual darkness. God moves in the deepest parts of our identity and produces fruit that spreads into our faith communities and throughout the world.

DEMONSTRATING PERSONAL FRUIT

God has created us as unique people. Personality and disposition mean that some fruit come easily for some persons. However, easily attainable fruit may cause us to lose sight of God's part in producing these fruit. We can begin to "pick" these fruit too often and become reliant on them as our favorite fruit category.

Other fruit may sit above our heads, just out of reach. There is good news about these fruit! Because these are "fruit of the Spirit" and not the "accolades of me," these hard-to-reach fruit represent opportunities for God to be at work in our lives. To help us reach these fruit we need to make space to develop them and surround ourselves with people who will hold us accountable.

In my time as a pastor, I have observed people who have surprised me when it comes to fruitfulness. For example, Mary had a friendly disposition, was well versed in Scripture, and active as the lay leader of the church. In one of our early conversations she gave me high praise saying, "You are exactly what this church needs to grow!" I thought the words were kind, but as time went on I heard members of the congregation express concerns about Mary. They approached me with frustrations about how Mary was trying to control people and was talking behind their backs.

Another example was Nick, who loved to sing. He was an exuberant, fast-moving man who had great ideas about the church. I can still remember him exclaiming, "Peter, if the church would just step out in faith we could do amazing things!" But Nick also had a domineering parenting style that was driving his children away. I learned that people such as Mary and Nick may not be as fruitful as I first thought.

However, I was surprised in a more positive way about other members in the churches I served. Two of my favorite examples are Ed and Vicki. Ed was a gruff man who said little, preferring to work with his hands. Nevertheless, Ed had a big heart for the youth of the church. We could always rely on him to help when the church hosted its vacation Bible school. Furthermore, when his long-dormant cancer resurfaced, he faced it with a peace that I had never previously witnessed.

Vicki was an energetic pianist. She led worship at one of the churches I was serving and willingly accepted any task we asked her to do. And yet, she was never controlling. She regularly tried to figure out how she could serve others.

Being fruitful is not about Bible knowledge or technical skill. As Robert Mulholland states in his book, *Invitation to a Journey: A Road Map for Spiritual Formation,* we read Scripture not for information, but for formation. Reading Scripture, praying, and practicing all the other spiritual disciplines are not activities to prove how good we are, but are ways to be with God. Fruitfulness is a measure of how well we love others out of our being loved by God. We stop trying to prove how good a Christian we are and instead focus on surrendering and trusting Jesus to lead us.

DEMONSTRATING FRUIT IN COMMUNITY

In recent years, the Indiana Conference has measured local church growth according to certain "vital statistics." Churches report the number of people in worship and the number of participants in small groups. The hope is that having these data will help a congregation improve its ability to produce fruit. The concept is that we work toward and achieve that which we measure. However, numbers by themselves do not necessarily signal fruit. God calls us to demonstrate fruit in our churches by changing the way people live.

Our social media culture does not help matters. People take snapshots and create posts that put the best spin on the story of their lives. They come to Facebook and compare themselves with others at their best. They rarely share their struggles and sacrifices because that would suggest failure. It is easier to shine light on accomplishments. Leadership author Jon Acuff reminds us that we should not compare our beginning to someone else's middle. Many churches make the mistake of comparing themselves to other churches. They risk getting caught up in a numbers game as they compare attendance figures, stewardship dollars, and the size of building programs. Churches need to seek the guidance of the Holy Spirit and ask: Where is Jesus leading our unique faith community?

The fruit of the Spirit centers on relationships. Relying on Jesus is a personal venture; yet it also leads us to being other-oriented. Martin Luther describes sin as a state of being bent in on oneself. Instead, when people rely on and abide in the Spirit of Jesus they find their hearts bending outward, toward others. Church leaders need to look for ways to move outside of the "holy huddles" and love the people in their community. Church teams and committees need to look outside of themselves. If we are not producing fruit and transforming lives, we need to ask a tough question: Are we getting in the way of God at work in our community?

The good news is that many churches are producing fruit in their communities. I know of a rural Indiana congregation whose members learned that seventeen thousand unchurched people lived in their region. This statistic shocked and inspired the congregation to move outside the walls of the church and provide care for the impoverished, offer a new style of worship, and create an outreach for at-risk youth. Worship attendance numbers soared in a community where the population was decreasing. Even more important was the visible fruit as lives were transformed.

DEMONSTRATING FRUIT GLOBALLY

In the early part of 2014, I went with the mission organization Operation Classroom to Sierra Leone, a beautiful country on the west coast of Africa. The people were warm and friendly in spite of their extreme poverty and the civic upheaval caused by a recent rebellion.

My colleagues and I visited Kissy Hospital, located in the capital city of Freetown. As we walked around the grounds, the director of Operation Classroom pulled us aside and pointed out a small creek bed. "Do you recognize that pile?" he asked. "That's the trash from this morning's breakfast. It pollutes the water, as does other sewage and medical waste. Conditions like these make Sierra Leone ripe for an epidemic."

The Ebola outbreak occurred a few months after my return home, prompting a missionary to observe: "When one person in Dallas becomes infected, we provide all sorts of resources. If Sierra Leone had a third of the resources spent on this one man, the outlook might be quite different."

What does it mean to see fruit in Sierra Leone? Being a fruitful disciple means that we are growing and making a difference in the lives of those who are in need. Is it possible to have goodness while ignoring poverty and social inequality? Throughout the centuries, God has been calling disciples into broken places. Disciples see poverty, political injustice, and social inequality as fertile soil for fruit. Tragedy and devastation do not have the final word. When we abide in Christ, God compels us into our community to connect with places where God has already been at work. After initial relief, organizations like Operation Classroom partner with others in Sierra Leone and provide practical help in education scholarships and vocational schools. Disciples, demonstrating fruit by stepping out in faith, see possibility where others see hopeless tragedy.

ABIDING IN CHRIST

God's grace is available for the deepest places of our souls. It includes the mistakes we make. It also includes a call to abide in Christ in an ongoing manner. It's not a one-time event. Every day offers opportunities to demonstrate fruit. Every moment provides opportunities to experience the Holy Spirit at work in us, in our churches, and in our world.

It took the enormity of ministry in my first appointment to bring up the big questions about my identity. I vividly remember the morning I drove to preach my first sermon in a congregation. As I wound around the serpentine back roads of Indiana, I experienced a moment of peace in the knowledge of who I am in Christ. I arrived in the gravel parking lot, scooped up my notes, and walked into church with the belief that I had nothing to prove. I only had Christ to share.

God offers us freedom when we move away from "works of flesh" to "fruit of the Spirit." We find fulfillment beyond what we thought was possible. Many voices compete for our attention and urge us in different directions. Yet, disciples find wholeness and fruit through the work of the Holy Spirit. God's grace is deeper and wider than we could ever know. When our primary motivation moves from our own preoccupation with our "selfish desires" to abiding in Christ, life takes a dramatic turn. When this happens, our lives and our world exemplify love, joy, peace, patience, kindness, goodness, faithfulness, gentleness, and self-control.

QUESTIONS

1. *Read Galatians 5:22-23. Which fruit are easier for you to demonstrate? How does God work through you to express them?*

2. *Which fruit are the most difficult for you to demonstrate? What would it look like for God to work through you to produce fruit in this area?*

3. *How do you see the fruit of the Spirit in your family?*

4. *Where do you experience the fruit of the Spirit in your congregation?*

5. *As you think about your community, where is God leading you and your congregation to demonstrate the fruit of the Spirit?*

RESOURCES

Bearing Fruit: Ministry with Real Results, by Lovett H. Weems Jr. and Tom Berlin. Nashville: Abingdon Press, 2011.

Five Practices of Fruitful Living, by Robert Schnase. Nashville: Abingdon Press, 2010.

Invitation to a Journey: A Road Map for Spiritual Formation, by M. Robert Mulholland, Jr. Downers Grove, IL: InterVarsity Press, 1993.

Life on the Vine: Cultivating the Fruit of the Spirit in Christian Community, by Philip D. Kenneson. Downers Grove, IL: InterVarsity Press, 1999.

Reaching Out: The Three Movements of the Spiritual Life, by Henri J. M. Nouwen. New York: Doubleday, 1975.

The Gift of Being Yourself: The Sacred Call to Self-Discovery, by David G. Benner. Downers Grove, IL: InterVarsity Press, 2004.

The Relational Soul: Moving from False Self to Deep Connection, by Richard Plass and James Cofield. Downers Grove, IL: InterVarsity Press, 2014.

CHAPTER 4

Shares in the Life and Witness of a Community of Disciples, including Baptism and the Lord's Supper

Jenifer Stuelpe Gibbs

"All the believers were united and shared everything. They would sell pieces of property and possessions and distribute the proceeds to everyone who needed them. Every day, they met together in the temple and ate in their homes. They shared food with gladness and simplicity. They praised God and demonstrated God's goodness to everyone." (Acts 2:44-47)

She invited me to her home for a small-group gathering from her church. She was a friend of a friend. I knew nothing of her church and little about her. Except for a few brief stints, I had never been a churchgoer. She seemed to sense that my life had run off the rails and asked me to stop by. When she described the meetings, they sounded like a throwback to the 1960s and I, with no bell-bottom pants, wasn't eager to attend. But I felt disconnected in my current city, so I took a chance and attended anyway.

Young professionals filled her house. They balanced paper plates of spaghetti on their knees while talking and laughing. As the meeting unfolded, members shared joys and concerns. I was surprised by their openness and shocked at the ways they worked to meet the needs of friends and strangers. Participants opened their Bibles, and I borrowed one. They discussed who God is and what God's story might mean for us. As they sang, joy spread across their faces.

I was uneasy when we broke into prayer groups. This was getting too personal. They turned and asked if they could pray for me. I nodded. They thanked God for my life and my attendance. They asked God to show me how beloved I am and how involved God is in my life. Unanticipated tears filled my eyes. I wondered what compels friends to stand with a stranger and ask that grand love be poured upon her. I left, only to return the next week. And the week after that.

The group's members were diverse. Our backgrounds and ideologies were different. Our roads to a shared community varied. Despite my reticence, my year with them changed me forever. By joining a circle of disciples seeking to follow Jesus, I became convinced that God's story was part of this world and part of my life.

ENTERING CAN BE CHALLENGING

The idea of participating fully in a community may challenge our sense of independence. We raise our children to be rugged individuals so they might survive and thrive in this world. Some of the best American success stories are about people who "pulled themselves up by their bootstraps." The irony is this: It takes a village to shape a child into a rugged individual. Teachers, coaches, and neighbors all have a hand in guiding our children toward adulthood. Many of us are those children.

The tension between the desire for independence and the need for community extends into our faith lives. Because we are part of a culture that values self-sufficiency, we often approach our faith journey as if we are traveling solo. We keep our questions to ourselves. We liken our religious journey to a personal quest. We may even view religious communities as vendors from which individuals can meet our needs, but we hesitate to immerse ourselves into the full life of the communities. We fail to understand that community is part of God's design.

Our Trinitarian God exists in one continuous community of being: Father, Son, and Holy Spirit. God is the source of our being, and we are made in God's image. Consequently our faith journey is tied to living with God and others. Early in the Bible it was the Israelites. Later, it was Jesus' twelve disciples. Then came the early churches formed after Jesus' resurrection. Today, Christian communities live out the same design in recovery meetings, strip malls or church buildings. Some communities live out God's transforming mission more gracefully or effectively than others, but we share one story. We are beautiful, gifted, imperfect, and often belligerent humans who are God's agents on earth. God works through us.

A UNIQUE WAY TO ENTER

Sunday morning. The faith community had gathered in the sanctuary for worship. A family came forward holding a four-month-old child. Her parents professed their faith in Jesus Christ. With the congregation as witnesses, they promised to raise their daughter in the community of disciples until she could make her own decisions about faith. Her body was squirmy and tense as her dad handed her to me, the unfamiliar woman in the white robe. I called her by name. Then I touched her forehead with water and baptized her. As I prayed, she leaned back into my arms and rested.

The faith community stood and pledged to support the child throughout her journey of faith. At that moment she stretched, yawned, and closed her eyes. She was asleep before I handed her back to her dad. Maybe the morning's milk had finally lulled her to sleep, or maybe deep in her spirit she understood she was at home. Throughout life she would join other groups. But through baptism, she entered a community of Christ's disciples all born of God's Spirit, and thus her extended family of God.

Families share life together in many ways. The same is true for the family of God. In Acts 2:37-39, the crowd asks, "What should we do?" Peter responds, "Each of you must be baptized in the name of Jesus Christ for the forgiveness of your sins. Then you will receive the gift of the Holy Spirit. This promise is for you." Thousands were baptized and began devoting themselves to fellowship.

The Greek word *koinonia* means fellowship, communion, or shared life (Acts 2:42-47). It provides a framework for how we participate in a community of disciples. Early disciples devoted themselves to being together, studying, sharing meals and prayers, worshiping, and serving those in need. United Methodists similarly practice sharing life but state it like this: We promise to faithfully participate by prayers, presence, gifts, service, and witness. This is the membership vow we take after we remember our baptism and affirm our faith. We vow to participate in community in these ways.

SHARING LIFE THROUGH PRAYER

While on a business trip, Mary felt flu-ish. It wasn't long before she was rushed to the emergency room. What followed were months of near-death experiences in intensive care. Her faith community, friends, and family prayed fervently for her. They sent e-mails to members of other faith communities across the country and world. Reflecting later, she discovered her growing sense of peace in the hospital coincided with the widening circle of prayers. To this day, she can't explain how her normally worried disposition relaxed into trust and peace. She has concluded that communities united in prayer are powerful. Through those community prayers, she found God to be trustworthy.

We hear countless stories of answered prayers for a single person as well as an entire region of a country. Over the past two thousand years, Scripture tells us that Jesus Christ has been interceding on our behalf (Romans 8:34). If Jesus can change the world in a few years of ministry and also rise from the dead, surely his prayers are powerful. I have to wonder what happens when two or two hundred join Christ in interceding for the needs of this world. Perhaps it helps change the world. But as author Philip Yancey suggests, most assuredly prayer changes us to be more like Christ. A disciple is one who participates in the prayers of the community.

SHARING LIFE THROUGH PRESENCE

When we become present in the community of disciples, we stand in solidarity. But any meaningful relationship requires us to engage something of ourselves. We can engage our thoughts, empathy, resources, or even our service. Being present, however, begins with showing up.

I remember when Mica began attending worship. She would slip in and out before anyone could approach her. When finally someone invited her to join a small group that would learn the prayer practice *Lectio Divina*, she replied, "Everyone here is so shiny. They have it together. I'm not shiny and neither is my life. Besides, I don't know anything about Christianity. I just like to come here sometimes." Maybe the dark chocolate and hot coffee were the draws. Whatever the reason, it wasn't long before honest conversations about life struggles emerged. Mica joined in. As the gatherings concluded, two group members let Mica know how important her perspective was to their experience of God. Mica's presence made a difference in her life with God, but also in the lives of others.

As we practice being present, we enter into one another's joys and suffering in unsuspecting ways. To remain present means we also embrace our differences and endure one another's flaws. Yet because God so loved us, we rely on compassion, kindness, humility, gentleness, and patience. We forgive one another as God has forgiven us (Colossians 3:12-13). Over time the connective threads of our shared humanity grow stronger and more apparent. We become trained in the ways of grace that we can apply to ever-widening circles of community. We are prepared to more readily and gracefully address the needs of others.

I have often heard it said that we tend to the needs of others as the "hands and feet of Christ." That phrase appears on more engraved church signs than I can count. Jesus Christ is the only incarnation of God, so we cannot literally be his hands and feet. However, those signs communicate a reality. Jesus Christ, now ascended, continues his ministry through the Spirit-filled community of disciples. We are the tangible body of Christ in this world (1 Corinthians 12:27). Although we are not the Incarnation, we can be incarnational. Through disciples, the Spirit can bear divine love, hope, and truth in this world. A disciple is one who practices presence in a community of disciples.

SHARING LIFE THROUGH GIFTS

The early community of disciples shared meals, belongings, and skills. They even sold some of their property to distribute the proceeds to those in need. The redistribution of wealth as a practice of faith equaled others such as studying the teachings of God, prayer, and meeting in the temple to worship. Sharing resources was and is integral to the life of faith and life in community.

Sharing resources takes practice. A student from a family of eight children wrote that his only wish was to receive a puppy for Christmas because then he would have something that was completely his. The youth had never known anything that he didn't have to share. At the end of the paper, he relented and said the whole family would enjoy his puppy, especially his little sister. The student was well-practiced at thinking about others. Sharing formed him in the ways of generosity and turned his eyes toward others. Practicing generosity is spiritual work.

Generosity, my husband says, requires us to change our orientation from ownership to stewardship. Owners address their own needs. Stewards are charged with caring for something that isn't ultimately their own. Through sacrificial sharing in community, whether money, time, or skills, we begin to understand that what we have is a gift to be given. Gifts used for God's work make a lasting impact. In the practice of sharing, we ultimately turn our eyes from our wants to the needs of others. God's focus becomes ours. A disciple is one who shares individual gifts with the community of faith.

SHARING LIFE THROUGH SERVICE

God's community extends outside the walls of our meeting places and often outside our comfort zones. Discipleship means serving throughout our daily lives, as expressed in chapter 5. When we serve singularly, others credit us as individuals for good works. Groups serving together point to something greater at work. When a community of disciples shows up to help repair homes in a violent neighborhood or opens a pantry to feed the hungry, then divine hope shines its brightest. Serving together displays the work of God unfolding now and into the future.

Holy Communion, also known as the Lord's Supper, reveals the past, present, and future work of God through Christ. It also instructs our participation in that work. Jesus Christ instituted Holy Communion for us. God is the host of the meal, and we are the invited guests. Taking part is both sign and symbol of God's work in this world. As we lift the bread and cup, we remember the past; Jesus' body and blood were sacrificed for the love of this world and all of us in it. In the present, we open our outstretched hands to receive the bread and cup for the forgiveness of sins and the nourishment of God's grace. As we watch others take Communion we glimpse the future.

The United Methodist tradition extends Holy Communion to everyone—the old and young, those who vote red or blue, and those of different races. We view the time as one of full reconciliation and peace. All receive the same bread and cup. We imagine when poverty will be no more. And finally, all who receive the elements receive the promise of sacrificial love and the power of resurrection now and forever. We envision a time when all tears are wiped away. We see the future for which God is working and we claim again that we are to be Christ's body and blood in the world. We know what to do. Because the meal began when we were served, we join God's work through serving others.

As the story goes, the folks in a certain community of faith disagreed about God's meal. Some questioned how the Communion table, which was gigantic, should be used. One side thought hosting their small community pantry from atop it, made sense. The other side thought piling canned goods, even for a community pantry, would desecrate the sacred space. Both make good cases. But the meaning of Communion directs us toward a clear choice. I imagine food piled high on a giant Communion table to feed all in need is one of the most Christlike uses of that table.

SHARING LIFE THROUGH WITNESS

The Bible is filled with accounts of ancient people's experiences with God. They declare God's story of love and justice and invite others to make that story their own. The Bible extends that invitation to all its readers. We continue that unfolding story as we bear witness to our experiences of God. Witnessing means we tell the story and also live it imaginatively and openly in our corners of the world.

One day I received a text from a community member who had experienced many losses in quick succession. Her message said, "Repeat the story of God's love and grace. I need to know it again." Filled with doubts, she was asking to hear the witness of God's reality. As she had over past months, she would stand on that witness as borrowed faith until she trusted God again. I was hesitant to witness to God in words let alone via text! It is easier to serve and let our deeds speak for themselves. Some of the best stories are silent and some have only words. The best and most vivid stories are both. So we take a chance. We share our stories in word and deed. We have no idea how our witness may further God's story. But it will; the Bible reminds us that witnessing always has.

A moment in a community of faith changed Don's life. While in high school, Don attended a retreat shortly after his girlfriend ended their relationship. At the opening session, a young man Don's age stood up and told his story. He was vulnerable and authentic in ways, as Don says, "sixteen-year-olds don't want to

49

be." The speaker described his many mistakes and how God helped turn his life around. Afterward, everyone was invited to go to the chapel to pray in silence. Don, still heartbroken, sighed and stared at the ceiling. "I know it sounds weird, but it was like the ceiling opened and a presence came down and sat beside me. I started to cry." It was Don's first personal encounter with God. After that experience, he started helping others. If God would come and meet him in his sadness, Don decided he should do the same. His relationship with God grew. Today, he still loves the prayers of silence in the gathered community. He waits and listens for God, who he knows will show up.

Because one boy shared his story about God, it forever changed Don's life. In turn, it has changed the lives of those Don serves. Witnessing in word and deed causes a beautiful domino effect. It is the means through which the story of God is offered as an invitation. A disciple is one who participates by witnessing throughout community.

QUESTIONS

1. *How has a community shaped your life or perspective?*

2. *Where do you see a hunger for connection and community in today's world? What changes of culture have helped create that deepening hunger?*

3. *What keeps you from entering a community of disciples more fully?*

4. *Of the community practices discussed, which ones do you regularly practice? Which ones would be areas of growth for you and your community?*

5. *Using this chapter as a foundation, how might you imagine the community of disciples playing a role in confronting social issues such as violence or poverty in your town or city?*

RESOURCES

I Am a Church Member: Discovering the Attitude that Makes the Difference, by Thom S. Ranier. Nashville: B&H Publishing Group, 2013.

The Awakening of Hope: Why We Practice a Common Faith, by Jonathan Wilson-Hartgrove. Grand Rapids, MI: Zondervan, 2012.

The New Parish: How Neighborhood Churches Are Transforming Mission, Discipleship and Community, by Paul Sparks, Tim Soerens, and Dwight J. Friesen. Downers Grove, IL: InterVarsity Press, 2014.

Prayer: Does It Make Any Difference? by Philip Yancey: Grand Rapids, MI: Zondervan, 2006.

Why I Am a United Methodist, by William H. Willimon. Nashville: Abingdon Press, 1990.

CHAPTER 5

Serves in Some Form of Ministry Every Day

Brian Durand

"Serve each other according to the gift each person has received, as good managers of God's diverse gifts." (1 Peter 4:10)

Did you ever pretend to be a superhero when you were a kid? You ran around the house pretending you were Spiderman, or Wonder Woman, or the Lone Ranger. When I was in grade school, I wanted to be Green Lantern. His ring could create whatever he needed to fight for justice and help people. I would use my fake Green Lantern ring to dash through the neighborhood saving the world.

As I look back, I realize that pretending to be a superhero was play. The desire to make a dramatic difference, though, to save the world around me, that part was real. Cartoons and comics made it look easy. One daring deed and you could save the world. One superpower or ability and you were equipped to make a difference.

As I was becoming a disciple, joining the church after college, I carried with me that desire to do something truly significant. I looked at my pastors and Mother Teresa and Martin Luther King

Jr. as models of discipleship for serving in ministry every day. Then I began to think: When God shows me how I can make a real difference like them, I'll jump at that opportunity to serve. When I know the Bible a little better, I'll be able to share with others. If I could just learn to do (fill in the blank), then I'll be ready to serve. All of these thoughts came from a desire to accomplish great things serving others for Christ, and all of these thoughts stood in the way of actually serving. I didn't realize at the time that our call from God as disciples isn't to perform great acts of service or be "faith superheroes." Our call is to regularly perform acts of love, serving in ministry every day.

To "serve in ministry every day" sounds daunting. Does this mean I need to volunteer with the church daily? What kind of ministry? How can I fulfill that obligation when I'm busy with work, or with my family, or searching for a job, or dealing with life's struggles? Where do I begin?

WHAT IS MINISTRY?

Ministry has many meanings. Buried among the definitions is one we shouldn't miss as we consider living in faith. Ministry is sharing in something or meeting someone's needs. We can do that—share in God's love and meet a neighbor's needs—every day. As a disciple, that is what we are called to do. We all are ministers, and ministry happens wherever we are and wherever we go.

Martin Luther referred to this idea as the priesthood of all believers. His biblical foundation came from 1 Peter 2:9: "But you are a chosen race, a royal priesthood, a holy nation, a people who are God's own possession. You have become this people so that you may speak of the wonderful acts of the one who called you out of darkness into his amazing light."

Too often church members today think that pastors and staff

are hired to do ministry on the congregation's behalf. We need to correct this misconception. The pastoral staff is hired to equip the disciples to "speak of the wonderful acts" of God and carry ministry into the world. Each disciple is uniquely gifted to glorify God in particular places and contexts—at work, at home, in the neighborhood, to those in a similar situation, to those facing a similar challenge. Our form of serving in ministry starts with who we are.

WHO WE ARE

In praising God, the psalmist sings, "You are the one who created my innermost parts; you knit me together while I was still in my mother's womb. I give thanks to you that I was marvelously set apart" (Psalm 139:13-14). God created you with unique gifts, talents, experiences, traits, and abilities, and set you apart. Pretty amazing to think about, isn't it? You've been given a toolbox for helping share God's love wherever you are.

One step in serving in some form of ministry every day is naming those "tools" in your toolbox. What experiences have shaped you that you may share with others? What talents do you have? What are you passionate about? What do others—friends, family—say are your gifts and talents? In 1 Peter 4.8-11, the hearer is invited to share the gifts given to bring honor to God in Christ Jesus:

> Above all, show sincere love to each other, because love brings about the forgiveness of many sins. Open your homes to each other without complaining. And serve each other according to the gift each person has received, as good managers of God's diverse gifts... that in everything God may be honored through Jesus Christ.

"Good managers" use the tools at their disposal for the greatest impact in their business, division, organization, and so forth. As a disciple, we manage God's diverse gifts by claiming them and using them in ministry every day. Our impact is praising and honoring God as we serve and share those gifts.

My great-aunt Edris lived in the community where I grew up. She had been a nurse before retiring and moving to a nearby assisted-living facility. She was feisty, incredibly intelligent, and knew the Bible better than anyone I've ever known, pastors included. As she reached her nineties, Aunt Edris would tell me occasionally that she wasn't much good to anyone, but it wasn't true. In fact, she taught Bible studies, challenged the minds of the other residents, and solved minor problems in her wing that the busy nurses didn't see. Because she shared the gifts, traits, and experiences in her toolbox, God ministered through her in ways that I don't think she even knew.

The truth is that regardless of our age—ten or thirty or sixty or ninety-eight—God has prepared us to share Christ's love with those around us. And it begins with claiming those tools—the life experiences, talents, gifts, and passions that make us who we are. What if God can use the tools in your life toolbox in ways you never imagined, right where you are?

WHERE WE ARE

I've always been fascinated by the biblical story of Esther. Did you know that the story never mentions God explicitly? Yet at the heart of the story is a deep truth that may explain why it is part of the Old Testament. It serves as a powerful example of how God is at work in and through us wherever we are.

For those who don't know the story, Esther is a Jewish woman who becomes queen of Persia. While she is queen, an advisor to the king recommends that all Jewish people be killed, according to royal decree. The king agrees and prepares the edict. Esther, at the risk of her own life, approaches her husband, the king, and requests that he withdraw the edict. By her act of courage, the Jewish people are saved.

Esther didn't set out to be a superhero. Instead, she finds herself as queen because of gifts from God—her beauty, personality, and family connections through her uncle Mordecai. She is at a pivotal place in the story of the Jewish people because of life circumstance. She is hesitant to act even then, but the encouragement of her uncle and an act of humility and spiritual discipline—fasting for three days—give her the courage to approach the king. Then two more God-given gifts, her intelligence and wisdom, help her guide the king toward the decision to save the Jewish people.

Esther's story presents a dramatic turning point as her uncle Mordecai says to her, "Who knows? Maybe it was for a moment like this that you came to be part of the royal family" (Esther 4:14).

What if God is saying something similar to us every day? What if God places us in certain situations or relationships so we can use our gifts and talents to make a difference? We are invited to claim these gifts, talents, and experiences and to recognize God's call to us where we are each day.

A former student of mine recently shared a powerful story of recognizing this call of God. He had made a commitment some time ago to follow God's nudges in his life. Through prayer and discernment, he decided that whenever he had an inkling that God's Spirit was encouraging him to act, he'd follow it. What happened after he made the commitment was a series of "ministry moments" that he couldn't have imagined. One day at an airport he felt the nudge to approach a woman and engage her in conversation. He introduced himself, and as soon as she learned he worked at a church, she poured out her soul, sharing a deep loss she recently had experienced. He was uncertain how to respond to her obvious pain but offered his condolences and suggested they pray together. The brief encounter brought comfort to the woman and affirmation to my student. He knew that God had used him right where he was, in the midst of the everyday, in a way he couldn't fathom or imagine.

LIVING IN FAITH EVERY DAY

In Deuteronomy 6:4-9, known in Jewish and Christian communities as the Shema, Moses presents God's word with the call to "Love the LORD your God with all your heart, all your being, and all your strength." Many who have been around the church for a long time know these words well. What follows, however, often is lost in the teaching. The passage continues:

> These words that I am commanding you today must always be on your minds. Recite them to your children. Talk about them when you are sitting around your house and when you are out and about, when you are lying down and when you are getting up. Tie them on your hand as a sign. They should be on your forehead as a symbol. Write them on your house's doorframes and on your city's gates.

In other words, share the love of God wherever you are every day. Share this love in your home and carry the words with you as a reminder wherever you go.

My wife, Cheryl, and I have friends who take time every day to pray with their two young boys. They read a story from a children's Bible, they exchange prayer requests, and then they pray. If anyone isn't feeling well or has a boo-boo (a regular occurrence in a home with preschoolers), they lay hands on him and pray. Not long ago they went on vacation with close neighbors who have a son about the age of their two sons. While traveling, they continued their family's practice of daily prayer. In the evening, after the three boys had spent a fun-filled day playing, the neighbor boy joined them for this time of prayer. He was usually quiet as he listened to the Bible story and then watched as the family prayed. Several days into their trip, the neighbor boy was out in the sun too long and had an uncomfortable sunburn. He was in some pain, and our friends didn't expect him to join them for evening devotions. The boy, however, wasn't going to miss the prayer time. He was so excited he had a sunburn because, as he told his parents emphatically, "Tonight I get to have hands laid on me for the prayer for my sunburn." When the families returned from vacation, the boy asked his mom and dad if they could read the Bible every night and pray like the other family, and they did.

God's call for the disciple to share God's love in the midst of everyday life is repeated throughout the Bible. In Jesus' parable of the good Samaritan, the Samaritan isn't overtly seeking to be a good neighbor. He is a good neighbor in the everyday path of his life and responds when he sees someone in need. In Acts 16, Paul and Silas witness where they are by not leaving their jail cells even after the earthquake opens the doors. In the Letter to the Hebrews the author urges readers to offer hospitality to the stranger or guest and encourages them to minister wherever they are, to whomever God brings across their paths, to be in ministry every day.

These stories serve as reminders that our work is a place where we perform ministry every day. Our homes are a place where we share in ministry every day. Our daily routines and life's interruptions create space where we can share in ministry every day.

At the first church I served, we launched a ministry initiative called Together in Ministry Everyday (TIME). A team of lay leaders began the initiative by asking everyone to commit to ninety minutes of service in ninety days. The invitation included a list of service opportunities in the community. In the next step, participants were encouraged not just to go out of their way to serve, but to begin to claim everyday opportunities to share God's love along their everyday paths in life.

WHERE DO I BEGIN?

Answering the call to serve as a disciple begins by saying yes to God. Eugene Peterson's paraphrase of Romans 12:1 in *The Message* offers this invitation, "So here's what I want you to do, God helping you: Take your everyday, ordinary life—your sleeping, eating, going-to-work, and walking-around life—and place it before God as an offering." What would it look like in your life to say yes to God at the start of each day? To pray that you may see the opportunities throughout the day to share Christ's love wherever you are and wherever you go?

Every Sunday at Clay Church, where I serve, we repeat in unison a covenant we call LIFE—Living in Faith Everyday.

I will pursue the faithful LIFE:
Reaching up to God each day,
Reaching out to serve someone this week,
And reaching one person with the love of God.

The covenant reminds us that in the week to come, we'll have opportunities to share God's love when we're in line at the grocery store or walking our dogs through the neighborhood. We'll have opportunities to serve our neighbors in the office on Wednesday morning or at the meeting scheduled for Thursday night. We'll encounter persons in our everyday paths who need us to share God's love with them.

Over and over the Bible attests that God calls on imperfect people, those in the midst of everyday life, those far from feeling they are superheroes. God calls on people who have unique passions and pet peeves and struggles and experiences and talents. And because of those gifts and where we are, we have the ability to stand on behalf of God's people, to cry out for justice, to heal the wounded, to feed the hungry, to offer hope, to pray for the person in our path who needs a word of truth and life. God calls us as disciples into places and spaces and times and experiences where we can use our gifts to share Christ's love.

We who say yes to following Christ are becoming his disciples. Imperfect? Yes. Superhero? No, at least not for me. Called by God? Yes. With tools in our toolbox? Yes. Searching for where God may use our tools to serve in some form of ministry every day? I hope so.

QUESTIONS

1. What gets in the way of your ability to imagine serving in ministry every day?

2. Make a list of the "tools" in your toolbox. What are your talents? What gifts do others recognize in you? What do you love doing? What are you passionate about?

3. Have you ever had a moment when you knew that God's Spirit was at work in or through you? How did this "moment of ministry" happen?

4. Write down your routine for a typical day. Looking through it, where do you see an opportunity to share Christ's love?

5. How could your church support ministry at home? At work? In the neighborhoods of those who come to worship?

RESOURCES

An Altar in the World: A Geography of Faith, by Barbara Brown Taylor. New York: HarperCollins, 2009.

APEST: Apostles, Prophets, Evangelists, Shepherds, Teachers (www.apesttest.com).

Called to Conquer: Finding Your Assignment in the Kingdom of God, by Derek Prince. Grand Rapids, MI: Chosen Books, 2010.

Dare to Dream: Creating a God-Sized Mission Statement for Your Life, by Michael Slaughter. Nashville: Abingdon Press, 2013.

Let Your Life Speak: Listening for the Voice of Vocation, by Parker J. Palmer. San Francisco: Jossey-Bass, 2009.

Spiritual Gifts Assessment (www.umc.org/what-we-believe/spiritual-gifts-online-assessment).

StrengthsFinder 2.0, by Tom Rath. New York: Gallup Press, 2007.

The Practice of the Presence of God, by Brother Lawrence. New York: Random House, 1977.

CHAPTER 6

Participates in God's Suffering and Transformation of the World

Brenda Freije

"All who want to come after me must say no to themselves, take up their cross daily, and follow me." (Luke 9:23)

When I was in sixth grade, the Indiana University women's tennis team played an exhibition match in my hometown of Fort Wayne. Two of my friends and I sat on the first row of the bleachers next to the courts. We watched every point and dreamed. We imagined hitting the ball with the same tremendous power, returning shot after shot with ease, and competing with similar grace. We wanted to play for a nationally ranked team like IU's, but were a long way from the Division I collegiate level. Fortunately, we had a coach who believed the dream was possible. He challenged us, and we practiced...a lot. Through hours of training and conditioning we learned to push ourselves to our limits. We learned how to compete and never give up. We learned the truth in the phrase "no pain, no gain." I didn't realize then how those important lessons would serve me well as I became a disciple of Christ.

Metaphors linking the life of discipleship with that of an

athlete are sprinkled throughout the New Testament. Disciples, like athletes, must practice and persevere if they are to overcome the inevitable obstacles they will encounter. Like most people, I would prefer to avoid life's painful struggles. No pain, no gain seems reasonable when training for sports but not for becoming a disciple. Still, discipleship requires us to participate in God's suffering and transformation of the world.

SUFFERING IS NOT A CHOICE

I chose to be an athlete and to engage in the physical struggle of training and competition. We typically do not have the luxury of choosing the struggles we will face in life. I work with people every day who endure suffering they neither expected nor deserved. As an example, a friend who lives with rheumatoid arthritis has to challenge herself daily to keep exercising or else her condition will worsen. She has discovered that if she runs a long distance, like a mini-marathon, her arthritic pain subsides for weeks after the run. Thus, periodically she forces herself to run long distances, giving in to the immediate pain of running, knowing that the benefits will be worth the effort in the end. My success as a tennis player pales in comparison to her successes each day to keep moving despite the aches and stiffness in her joints.

Pain and loss are regular parts of life. Devastating events such as hurricanes, floods, tsunamis, illness, disease, and untimely deaths cause us to ask why. At some point, we all suffer—some more than others. Yet sometimes our human suffering is unnecessary.

I recently heard the story of Sarah, a young woman who ran away from home as a teenager and became a prostitute. Sarah's father sexually molested her as a child, telling her that he loved her and this is how people show love. As Sarah's story unfolded, I grew angrier and angrier. How could a father mistreat his daughter this way? Could Sarah, torn apart by abuse and prostitution, hope to experience healing and wholeness? Was it possible for her to find her way out of her pain?

WE HAVE CHOICES

The Ebola virus has claimed thousands of lives in West Africa, inflicting incredible suffering on medical workers, communities, and families. The world is feeling the effects of Ebola as countries impose travel restrictions, hospitals train for the potential arrival of Ebola victims, and scientists work frantically to develop a vaccine against this deadly virus. Jesus' counsel to his disciples that following him will be costly takes on a new depth of meaning with Ebola in mind. The Apostle Paul emphasizes the risks when he writes to the Corinthians about the hardships he was enduring so that more people would come to know the hope and love of Jesus. Both Jesus and Paul focus our attention on the choices we have to make. To be a disciple means to participate in, and even embrace, the struggles of life. Christ calls all of us into his community, but we each must make the decision to follow and form our lives after Christ.

Why make the choice to follow? Wouldn't life be easier if we chose a different path? I don't think so. Christ did not come to save a perfect world where Ebola viruses don't exist, people aren't hungry, children do not experience violence, communities are not oppressed, terrorists do not fly planes into buildings, and wars never break out. If hardships do not impact you directly, talk with others. Someone close to you has likely been affected. Christ's work and message point to the greater truth reflected in the title of this chapter—that we are called to participate in God's suffering because those are the places that need Christ's hope, love, and transformation.

SUFFERING: A SEEDBED

Suffering is a seedbed of transformation. It is a place where new life is made possible. When we lose, we can gain greater life. Sometimes that new life has little to do with physical changes around us and has everything to do with our spiritual depth. Greg Clapper writes in his book *When the World Breaks Your Heart* about the crash of United Airlines Flight 232 in 1989, which killed 113 people. As a National Guard chaplain, he had a firsthand account of the tragic event and its aftermath. He describes how Teresa, an office worker, was called to help at the crash scene. At the time, Teresa was living in a destructive marriage and struggling with alcohol abuse and low self-esteem. Having no crisis intervention or medical training, she found herself working for hours providing aid among the wounded and dead. Later, as she recalled the events of the crash, she began to examine the broken places in her life. In coping with the trauma, she found she could cope with her own suffering. Teresa could begin to imagine the possibilities of new life. Clapper notes that tragedies like plane crashes can snap us out of our stupors, push us to name our broken places, and seek new life. Take up your cross.

Sarah, the young woman who ran away from home to escape her father's abuse, experienced a similar transformation. She assumed she would die on the streets, a victim of her violent environment. One night, Sarah met Anne, a former prostitute who had found a new life and now worked to help other women leave the streets. Anne began meeting with Sarah regularly. They talked about Sarah's life, her abuse, and the dreams she once had. Slowly, Sarah began to believe that she was worthy of real love, that she didn't need to sell her body, that she deserved better. Transformation took root and grew. Sarah is now married with a family. She also works the streets to free other prostitutes from the bondage of their trade. Take up your cross.

NOT ALL SUFFERING LEADS TO TRANSFORMATION

Suffering and transformation go together, but not all suffering leads to transformation. Some choose not to take up their cross. Others become exhausted in the effort. Unfortunately, most of us will encounter persons in our lives who have experienced tragedy and come out the other side bitter and hard. Who can blame them? Struggle reveals the reality of our vulnerability, and sometimes that reality is too much to bear. So, why do some people cope with suffering by growing more spiritual, self-aware, and God-centered while others do not? Our understanding of God and our willingness to embrace the theology of the cross may play a role.

It is easy to view suffering as something distinct from God—as if God has abandoned or forgotten us. In reality, God suffers with us just as God has suffered with all of creation throughout history. The Israelites in the Old Testament exemplify this. Enslaved in Egypt, the Israelites cried out to God at the injustice of being subjected to backbreaking work and the whims of Pharaoh. God responded and worked to deliver the people through any means necessary. Hardly the distant ruler, God entered into the hurtful situation and made it God's own. God suffered too.

I lift up this example from the Old Testament because too often God in the Old Testament is perceived as distant and uncaring, even violent and vengeful. Yes, the Old Testament contains troubling passages that seem to demonstrate these characteristics in God. The sweep of God's story from the Old Testament to the New Testament, however, points to a loving and compassionate God.

God's suffering is no less real today than it was with the Israelites. God cares for all who suffer and extends compassion universally. Not everyone understands or accepts it, however. As disciples, we have the joy of knowing, like the Israelites, from whom the

69

compassion comes. When a friend visits us in the hospital after a surgery, shows up at our doorstep with a meal to feed our family while we are sick, or sends a card on the anniversary of a loved one's death, God's love and compassion become evident. We are never forgotten. As disciples we have the comfort of knowing that we are formed in God's image, an authentic and loving relatedness exists between us, and God will work through whatever means possible to comfort us.

The power of presence

As part of my seminary education, I completed clinical pastoral education (CPE) in a hospital working as a chaplain. In the classroom we learned how to care for the dying; in the hospital we heard firsthand from several medical professionals who work with hospice patients. Listening to them describe their call to be a loving presence to those who are dying was life-giving. Being present in the midst of suffering can bring comfort.

Larry and Carole Prible, dear friends of our family, have created a foundation called Love at Work Ministries, which provides assistance in the poverty-stricken urban slums of Alajuelita, Costa Rica. Larry and Carole became acquainted with Alajuelita when they attended a meeting for the Habitat for Humanity International Board on which Larry served. The meeting was held near Alajuelita, a place Habitat for Humanity did not serve because the city's infrastructure was so broken that Habitat's model of home building could have little impact. Larry and Carole were heartbroken by the condition of the slums. They could not forget the faces of the children they encountered. They had to do something.

Love at Work operates on the principle that our love must be more than talk. True love shows itself in words and action.

Love at Work has had plenty of action. In the past six years the nonprofit organization has worked with local residents to build homes and a school, feed the hungry, reach hundreds of children and youth through camping programs, and form a church. The impact has been great, but the need is tremendous because few job opportunities exist for all the people living in the area. Given this reality, it is easy to question why Larry and Carole dedicate so much of their time to this seemingly forgotten part of the world. When asked about this, Larry might tell you the story of a woman living in a dirt-floor home that floods with mud when it rains. She and her son were unable to travel to find food for several days during a period of nonstop rain. They were losing hope. Miraculously, volunteers from Love at Work were able to reach them with food despite the conditions. Incredibly grateful, the woman explained how she had prayed and prayed to God for help, but God didn't seem to be listening. She thought God had forgotten them. Now she knew God remembered them. Why is Love at Work in Alajuelita? Because nobody should ever feel forgotten. Even when situations appear hopeless, participating in God's suffering like Larry and Carole can change the world by affirming God's loving presence.

TAKING UP OUR CROSS IS RISKY

Becoming a disciple is a risky venture. Participating in God's suffering will likely place us in harm's way more often than we imagined. A simple survey of mission trips and work projects that United Methodists across the country undertake each year reveals some of the risks. It may sound adventurous to serve the needy in places such as Africa, Appalachia, and the urban centers of the United States, but such trips can be dangerous, even life-threatening. Larry and Carole Prible, lifelong residents of Indianapolis, never imagined they would spend half of their retirement years working tirelessly in a remote, inner-city slum in Costa Rica where crime, violence, and illness run rampant. Why participate?

I was recently struck by the power of this question when listening to a young man from Sierra Leone talk about working in the Ebola ward at a local hospital. Ebola attacked the young man and his entire family. His parents and his siblings were laid on beds near one another in the ward. Within days they all died. Only the young man survived. Hardly able to imagine his pain, a reporter asked him how he could work among so much death and tragedy. The young man replied that caregivers had risked their lives to save him, so he has to do the same. Other workers in the ward described how the young man's experience and testimony were transformative for patients battling the virus. Most assume there is no hope. When they find out that he survived Ebola, they are more willing to fight for their own lives. Out of tragedy, hope can live in the form of a young Ebola survivor who has lost everyone he loves yet found a way to serve using his experience to help others.

TAKING UP OUR CROSS REQUIRES PRACTICE

When we make the choice to be disciples, a choice we may have to renew regularly, the Gospel of Luke reminds us to practice. We have to take up our cross "daily" so that it becomes routine and habitual (Luke 9:23).

A few summers ago, I started running for exercise, something I could do while waiting at the soccer fields for my kids to finish practice. The first several weeks of running were painful experiences. After ten minutes I wanted to stop or at least walk. I kept at it and now running distances feels natural, even something I long to do. Our spiritual health requires the same kind of repetition and perseverance. We take up our cross daily to stretch and build our cross-bearing muscles so that when we really need to be strong, we can do the heavy lifting.

How do we take up our cross daily? A story from the Gospel of Matthew gives some clear guidance. In Matthew 25:31-46 we read about sheep and goats and how God will someday separate us into two groups like a shepherd separates his flock. The sheep inherit the kingdom prepared for them while the goats are instructed to depart. Who are the "sheep"? According to Matthew, they are the ones who fed the hungry, gave water to the thirsty, welcomed the stranger, clothed the naked, cared for the sick, and visited the prisoners. They did these things out of love and compassion for their neighbor not knowing that God was aware. The "goats" ignored the needs of their neighbors. They did not care for others, only themselves.

I find it interesting that the sheep in Matthew's story are invited to share in God's kingdom when I believe they already were. I hope you've had the experience of helping someone in need and reflected on how you were impacted. Anytime we alleviate suffering, we experience and share in God's kingdom and dream for all of creation.

The judgment reflected in this Matthew story is convicting. I have to ask myself, How often do I participate in activities that ease the suffering of others? Is it a natural response or something I have to remind myself to do? We need to take up our cross "daily," participating in the world's suffering regularly so that it becomes easier. Like the basketball player who does not have to think about how to shoot a free throw, our action only becomes a habit through repetition. Otherwise, we are likely to revert to our natural tendency to worry about our own needs, rather than the needs of someone else.

What happens when the suffering is our own and not someone else's? Suffering takes on new meaning when we feel like Christ on the cross crying out, "My God, my God, why have you forsaken me?" (Mark 15:34 NRSV). Somehow we have to figure out how to cope with the pain while struggling with the question of why we are facing it at all. There are no easy answers in these situations. Yet, in the middle of the struggle, we may catch a glimpse of the truth we can learn from those who have suffered much... every struggle is an opportunity for spiritual growth.

It Comes Down to Hope

In sixth grade, when my two best friends and I watched the Indiana University women's tennis team compete, we hoped someday to be as good as they were. So we trained and struggled and dedicated the time and energy necessary to perfect our games with the support of our coach, our parents, and many others along the way. It worked. One of my friends received a scholarship to play for the University of California at Santa Barbara, my other friend received a scholarship to play for Miami of Ohio, and I received a scholarship to play for Indiana University.

Why do we choose to participate in the struggles of life? It is an act of faith and hope similar to that of an athlete who keeps pressing toward a goal. God is in the midst of all of our lives—even in the athletic endeavors of three teenagers. Our joys are God's joy. Our suffering is God's suffering, wherever it is occurring, whether across the world or across the hall. The practice of participating in God's suffering helps us learn to trust the story of the gospel and God's transforming power to do wonderful things, even in the midst of bleak circumstances. As people who celebrate resurrection, we cannot shut our eyes to the suffering around us, otherwise our talk of resurrection rings hollow. Through this discipleship practice we participate in the hope of resurrection and take part in God's kingdom that is here and still coming.

QUESTIONS

1. *Think about a time when you experienced personal suffering. How did it make you feel?*

2. *How did those around you respond to your suffering? In what ways was it helpful?*

3. *Who in your community is suffering? What could you do to comfort them or provide assistance? What risks do you take in reaching out with compassion?*

4. *Where have you seen or experienced God's transformation in the midst of suffering? How did you respond?*

5. *The Luke text at the beginning of the chapter calls for us to take up our cross daily. What daily acts might you adopt to help you build your cross-bearing muscles?*

RESOURCES

Falling Upward: A Spirituality for the Two Halves of Life, by Richard Rohr. San Francisco: Jossey-Bass, 2011.

Lament: Reclaiming Practices in Pulpit, Pew, and Public Square, Sally A. Brown and Patrick D. Miller, editors. Louisville: Westminster John Knox Press, 2005.

Living with Contradiction: An Introduction to Benedictine Spirituality, by Esther de Waal. Harrisburg, PA: Morehouse Publishing, 1997.

No Pain, No Gain: Hope for Those Who Struggle, by John R. Wimmer. New York: Ballantine Books, 1985.

Trauma + Grace: Theology in a Ruptured World, by Serene Jones. Louisville: Westminster John Knox Press, 2009.

When the World Breaks Your Heart: Spiritual Ways of Living with Tragedy, by Gregory S. Clapper. Nashville: Upper Room Books, 1999.

CHAPTER 7

Anticipates a Future Life in the Presence of God

Kimberly King

"I write these things to you who believe in the name of God's Son so that you can know that you have eternal life." (1 John 5:13)

The conversation was lively and focused on individual and shared memories. As I knocked on the door and came into the room, I heard recollections of family dinners, funny stories, and significant events. I'd been there several times now, enough that we were on a first-name basis. Over the past week, Maggie had drifted in and out of consciousness. Sometimes she seemed to be living in the past, recalling moments experienced long ago. Other times she seemed fully present with her appropriate responses peppered with dry humor and delivered with perfect timing. And then again, there were times when she seemed to know of some future yet unrevealed to those in the room with her.

The hospital staff had called Maggie's family to gather to say their final goodbyes. They'd been standing a constant vigil at her bedside for the past three days. As Maggie's respiration continued to slow, they asked the obvious questions. "How long does she have? Do you think she's close? Can she still hear us?" I had no solid answers, so I encouraged the family to take a break. They left to get some lunch and were gone for about an hour.

In that hour, I traveled with Maggie as she visited some otherworldly place, having lively conversations with people whose names I didn't recognize. She visited with John and with Helen and with Madge. She said things like "I'm not ready. I see it. Oh, that's beautiful. Okay." I can only imagine what the other side of those conversations might have been. It felt to me as though they were beckoning her to someplace amazing. She was clearly in a real conversation with people I could neither hear nor see. Abruptly she ceased speaking. I could barely sense her breathing. But she seemed comfortable, content, and calm. The moment was holy.

Maggie's family members returned to the room. She sensed their presence, rearranged herself in the bed, and as is common during the dying process Maggie rallied once more. Opening her eyes fully she made direct eye contact with each person who surrounded her bed, and said softly to each one, "I love you." Then she closed her eyes, and died.

DEATH IS INEVITABLE

The circle of earthly life, as we know it, begins with conception and ends with death, something we must all face. As a pastor and a therapist, I spend a lot of time caring for and being present with people as they experience difficult and challenging circumstances. Often I am with families as they say their final goodbyes, prepare to honor the lives of their loved ones, and then begin the difficult task of creating new lives for themselves without their loved ones. These, and most life-changing events, are commonly accompanied by questions about the meaning of life in the presence of God. Those questions explore the significance of life on earth and in heaven. Some people are sure of the afterlife, and their faith is strengthened by loss, grieving, and accepting the mystery of death. Others experience a crisis of faith and question the existence of God and the possibility of a future life. The transformation that emerges from the painful suffering and crises of faith that frequently accompany the death of a loved one is sacred.

DEATH MAKES US UNCOMFORTABLE

Why does talking about death make us so uncomfortable? Perhaps it's fear of the unknown. None of us really knows for sure what death is like. Perhaps it's a hope that we can avoid death since we live in a time when medicine and science are able to prolong and even restore life.

I'm also confronted with the fact that individuals and communities in our culture often have difficulty dealing with death and the grief and mourning that follow. Such painful times remind us of what could happen to us. How often have you heard someone ask, "Shouldn't she be over it by now?" Or, "Be strong." Organizations perpetuate this myth that we should compress our mourning and quickly "get over it," by administering policies that offer us three days of bereavement leave from our places of employment, even for our most significant losses.

Scripture and United Methodist tradition teach us to look with hope and anticipation to the resurrection made possible by Jesus' death on the cross. But, focusing on the future may rob us of the good work that grief and mourning can do in us and in our community right now. Journeying through grief with the companionship of other disciples can bring us to a place where we can again make sense of the world. Denying ourselves the opportunity to experience intense sorrow might rob us of the opportunity to be in relationship with one another in the way that Jesus was in relationship with his distressed disciples.

DEATH OF JESUS

Prior to his own death Jesus gathered with the disciples. "Don't be troubled," he said. "Trust in God. Trust also in me." He went on to tell the disciples that there was no need to be troubled, because he was going to prepare a place for them. And that he would return and take them to be with him (John 14).

Still, the Gospels tell us that the disciples were "troubled." Mortality is frightening. Even for Jesus who knew that his death was inescapable. He faced this fear by talking with God. Jesus prayed for God's will to be done, and asked also whether he could avoid the cross. "Father, if it's your will, take this cup of suffering away from me. However, not my will but your will must be done" (Luke 22:42).

Jesus promised to prepare a place for his disciples and to accompany them to that place, a promise made to all disciples of Jesus Christ! And it is a good reason for us to anticipate a future life in the presence of God. Typically, we think of this future life in the presence of God as the eternal life we will experience after our death. And that is highly appropriate. However, a disciple has a hope that transcends death. Jesus said, "Whoever hears my word and believes in the one who sent me has eternal life and won't come under judgment but has passed from death into life" (John 5:24). This hope, of passing from death into life, is a disciple's present reality!

DISCIPLES HAVE A HOPE BEYOND DEATH

Paul speaks of this eternity given to believers in his Letter to Titus. "I'm sent to bring about the faith of God's chosen people and a knowledge of the truth that agrees with godliness. Their faith and this knowledge are based on the hope of eternal life that God, who doesn't lie, promised before time began" (Titus 1:1-2). The hope expressed in this passage is not wishful, but expectant and confident, because it rests on the promise of a God who does not lie. Eternal life is not simply something disciples will possess someday, but something available right now through trust in a risen Savior.

Disciples celebrate this hope in worship. We acknowledge the power of Jesus' resurrection each week when we celebrate the transformative power of our relationship with a risen Savior. We join together in worship of the living Lord because we hope to experience the transforming power of Christ's resurrection in our daily lives. It is part of the yearning for a lost communion. We need to participate both individually and corporately in worship to nourish ourselves for what life brings in the coming week. We fulfill our need to connect with God and with others, and we move from emptiness toward fullness, as we gather each week seeking restoration, renewal, and resurrection.

A HOPE IN RESURRECTION

After Jesus' body had been moved from the cross to a borrowed tomb, several of his female followers prepared burial spices. Sunday, the third day following Jesus' death, the women went to the tomb to anoint Jesus' body. They found the stone that covered the entrance to the tomb rolled away. They did not find Jesus' body inside the tomb. But, according to Matthew 28:5-7, an angel appeared and said to the women:

> Don't be afraid. I know that you are looking for Jesus who was crucified. He isn't here, because he's been raised from the dead, just as he said. Come, see the place where they laid

81

him. Now hurry, go and tell his disciples, "He's been raised from the dead. He's going on ahead of you to Galilee. You will see him there." I've given the message to you.

Over and again, Scripture celebrates the resurrection of Jesus Christ and confirms his resurrection was a historical event that many witnessed. John's Gospel reports that Jesus appeared and stood among the disciples, offered them his peace, and showed them the crucifixion wounds on his hands and side. "When the disciples saw the Lord, they were filled with joy" (John 20:20). Paul describes numerous people who also witnessed the resurrected Jesus including Cephas, "more than five hundred brothers and sisters at once," James, and himself (1 Corinthians 15:3-9).

A BELIEF IN RESURRECTION

Books chronicling near-death experiences are popular and numerous. The authors are a diverse group. Some are religious, others are not. Some are young, some are old. Their vocations and life-experience are wide-ranging. Many of the accounts are anecdotal, but others claim research as their basis. Many tell of bright lights, warmth, weightlessness, music, hallways and rooms that seem to never end, and a feeling of complete peace and love. While not all reports are of positive experiences, overwhelmingly these accounts support that what appears to be the end of a journey is really the beginning of another journey.

I can't prove it, but I believe that Jesus lived, was crucified, died, and was buried. I believe Jesus rose from the dead, talked with and comforted his followers, and gave them instruction about how to love one another and live together in covenant community. That's pretty preposterous! I'm not aware of any scientific method that "proves" what Christians claim. My point is not to prove anything, but to awaken curiosity about why it matters that disciples of Jesus

Christ have a hope that promises them a future life in the presence of God.

It matters because this belief and this hope are guideposts for daily living. A future life in the presence of God can begin right now!

My seminary training included work as a hospital chaplain on an oncology unit. Every day I visited with patients who were dying. Dying people often talk about the meaning of their lives in relationship to people to whom they feel closely connected. When life is precariously unpredictable, and time is limited, we talk about how we have offered and received love. We remember with regret withholding love, and we have a better understanding of unconditional love. We find new appreciation of the people we call family, friend, and faith community. It is through these relationships that we experience God's love in our lives. When we offer love, we can become clear about our purpose. When our purpose is clear, we are better at discerning the meaning of our lives as disciples.

As disciples who have been saved by grace, we do not neglect earthly life. We use it to practice for eternal life. As Paul says, disciples are "God's accomplishment, created in Christ Jesus to do good things. God planned for these good things to be the way that we live our lives" (Ephesians 2:10). Disciples live in ways that embrace practices that strengthen body, mind, and spirit. Part of this lifelong venture is to live in ways that illustrate what it looks like to love God and to love our neighbor as ourselves.

Living in God's presence

What I knew about Charlene was that she was "a single woman by choice." She was fairly emphatic when she told me how she had chosen a career in the city to escape her small rural town. She had enjoyed a career in accounting and had loved living in the city for the past seventy years. She'd witnessed many changes since living in her first tiny urban apartment. At age ninety-four she still lived independently, drove a car, played in a chamber orchestra, and danced at least once a week with the people in her ballroom dancing club. All these activities paled next to her commitment to deepening her spiritual life. She read the Bible every day and rarely missed Sunday school. This had been her practice for fifty years. She often would say she had no fear of death. The story she told me explained her fearlessness.

For several weeks, Charlene had reminded me she wanted to share with me something she'd experienced many years before, shortly after the death of her parents. We decided to meet at a restaurant and celebrate her ninety-fourth birthday.

Charlene began her story explaining that the event she was recounting took place when she was at a critical time in her career and had just received a promotion, which in her day was uncommon for a woman. A call from her parents quickly deflated her sense of accomplishment and joy.

Her parents wanted her to return home to care for them. She was their only child. Her mother was ill and her father was unable to care for her without help. "I agonized after that call," Charlene said. "I desperately wanted to stay in the city, but I cared deeply about my parents." She went on to tell me that she dropped to her knees and prayed for guidance, a practice she always followed in times of doubt. Her prayer went something like this: "Lord, you know best. I trust you to be with me and my parents." After that prayer, she said she left everything in God's hands.

A few days later, she decided she would move back home. As she was working out the details, Charlene received another phone call. The caller identified himself as a state trooper. Her parents had died in a one-car auto accident. Charlene was incredibly grief-stricken. She had not had a chance to say a final goodbye.

In the midst of her anguish, as well as her deep trust in God, Charlene was alone with the caskets of her parents for a private viewing prior to the funeral. As she sat there, she said, "The most amazing thing happened." She became very animated in describing for me "swooshes of bright warm light" that seemed to come through the walls, race across the room, then fill the space with a light brighter than she'd ever seen before or since. She said, "It was strange. The light was bright, but not blinding." In the light she saw her parents and they were happier than she'd ever seen them. The memory remained with Charlene as though it happened yesterday. More than the visual memory was the emotional memory of "feeling totally at peace." What happened that day assured her that Jesus has prepared a place for his disciples. She said that no matter what unfortunate things had happened, she could be thankful because, for a few moments, she had experienced a future in the presence of God. This experience had assured her that her own future in God's presence was secure and irrevocable.

Charlene is one example of a disciple who places Jesus and his teaching at the center of her life. She practices accepting others as Jesus accepts her. She embraces the mystery of death as she waits for the funeral of her parents. She faces fear with confident faith, fervent prayer, hope for and assurance in things yet unseen (Hebrews 11:1). She says this has worked for ninety-four years.

In my experience as a pastor I've stood with many people as they transitioned from this life to the next. The sacredness of dying assures me that disciples of Jesus Christ can anticipate a future life in the presence of God. It also convinces me that we must always move into the future with joyful and expectant confidence in God's promise of eternal life.

QUESTIONS

1. What is difficult about discussing death?

2. Is it important for disciples to discuss death and eternal life? If so, why?

3. What are the ideas about death that are prominent in your family and faith community?

4. What does a future life in the presence of God evoke for you?

5. How can you embrace eternal life by the way you live your life now?

RESOURCES

Calendar: Christ's Time for the Church, by Laurence Hull Stookey. Nashville: Abingdon Press, 1996.

Evidence of the Afterlife: The Science of Near-Death Experience, by Jeffrey Long MD with Paul Perry. New York: HarperOne, 2010.

Finally Comes the Poet: Daring Speech for Proclamation, by Walter Brueggemann. Minneapolis: Fortress Press, 1989.

Proof of Heaven: A Neurosurgeon's Journey into the Afterlife, by Eben Alexander. New York: Simon & Schuster, 2012.

Shared Wisdom: Use of the Self in Pastoral Care and Counseling, by Pamela Cooper-White. Minneapolis: Augsburg Fortress Press, 2004.

Stages of Faith: The Psychology of Human Development and the Quest for Meaning, by James W. Fowler. San Francisco: HarperSanFrancisco, 1981.

CHAPTER 8

Yearns to Lead Others to Become Disciples

David Williamson

"Come, follow me, . . . and I'll show you how to fish for people."
(Matthew 4:19)

I was a sophomore in high school, attending a student leadership conference in Minneapolis that focused in part on equipping teens to share their faith with others. The conference leaders gave us religious tracts and instructed us on how to explain the "Four Spiritual Laws." We learned that the eternal fate of others depended on us sharing this faith with them (but if they rejected the faith we shared, then whatever happened in eternity was on their own heads). Then we boarded buses that dropped off at various points around the city to practice our skills on unsuspecting bystanders. The bus I boarded took us to the zoo.

I spent most of the day hanging back, trying to muster up the courage to speak to someone. I must've approached a dozen people, only to turn away at the last second. I don't know why I ultimately chose a certain dad with his family as my target. If I'd understood what I know now—that creating the time and space to go to the zoo with your family is a sacred thing for a dad—then I'm sure I wouldn't have bothered him. But maybe it was *because* he was with his family that he seemed nice and fatherly, and I thought he would be a safe person to approach.

I was wrong. No sooner had I started to introduce myself than he cut me off. "If I had a shotgun right now," he seethed through clenched teeth, "I'd blow the heads off all you Christians." No doubt many of my colleagues had approached him throughout the day, and he was fed up. Well-meaning but intrusive teens were ruining what was supposed to have been a pleasant outing with his kids. And he let me know it.

After that, I couldn't bring myself to talk to anyone else. I placed my tracts in a public place where they might be picked up and read and headed to the gathering point to get back on the bus. That evening in worship, conference leaders celebrated the total number of people who had received Christ that day through our collective efforts. But as I heard the news, I couldn't help feeling a sense of failure. Certainly part of my feeling was because I hadn't contributed at all to that total count. Even beyond that, though, I felt like I'd participated in something that wasn't *good*, and I wondered if we did more to repel people from Christ than to attract them.

THE RISK OF EVANGELISM

While most Christians don't have the experience of being threatened by a shotgun, we nonetheless feel a similar sense of "danger" when it comes to sharing our faith. We might offend the person with whom we are talking, or perhaps we'll bring discomfort into a friendship that has been easy and smooth up to that point. There is a very real social risk of rejection and estrangement.

Simply put, sharing the good news doesn't feel very good for many of us.

As a result, most followers of Jesus express their faith only when surrounded by others who share that same faith. The longer people are "in" the church, the less likely they are to develop friendships with those who are outside the faith, so that even if persons *wanted* to share their faith, they wouldn't know with whom. Pastors rarely preach or teach about evangelism, because congregants don't like being pushed into uncomfortable territory. And the results of this are staggering. In the last two years for which we have statistics (2011–13), membership in The United Methodist Church in the United States declined by 181,630, and average worship attendance fell by 113,142. In that same period, almost half of United Methodist congregations failed to report a single member who joined by "profession of faith."

All this is in stark contrast to the calling and mission Jesus gave his disciples. When Jesus called his first disciples—Peter and Andrew—he promised them that they would learn to "fish for people" (Matthew 4:19). Likewise, his final commission to the disciples was to "go and make disciples of all nations" (28:19). The church has become like that old sermon illustration of the "fisherman's society" that lost its way. At their weekly meetings the members would spend time recounting the great tales of the fishermen of old, reviewing all the latest fishing gear to hit the market, and sharing tips on how to enhance one another's fishing technique, and so forth. Over the years, they developed close friendships and meaningful traditions and took great care to pass these connections on to future generations of their society. Yet in all this activity, one essential thing was forgotten—no one actually fished anymore.

So how do we recover? How do we wake the sleeping giant of the church? Truth be told, I'm not sure. I am sure it will require no less an outpouring of God's Spirit than occurred on the original day of Pentecost. But short of that, here are a few thoughts that might help reframe the practice of evangelism within the life of Christian discipleship.

EVANGELISM IS A *GOOD* WORD

In our culture many associate the word *evangelists* with slick preachers on TV with far too much makeup and far too many empty promises. Or some may associate *evangelicals* with a particular group of Christians with a particular political agenda. Both words, though, are rooted in the Greek word *euangelion*, which simply means "good news." The heart of evangelism is bearing the good news of Jesus' love and grace to a world that sorely needs it.

In their book *Outflow*, Steve Sjogren and Dave Ping make the helpful point that to bear good news to our neighbors, we must first *be* good news to them. By that they mean that we need to be the kind of neighbors (or customers, or bosses, or clients, or coworkers) that people like having around. They smile when they see us coming around the corner, because they know good news is on the way. The more the world sees us as people of hope, people who embody God's love and patience and good will, the more ready they will be to hear the message we bear.

EVANGELISM IS A *RELATIONAL* ACTIVITY

A friend recently showed me a YouTube video poking fun at Christians. The "preacher" in the scene talks about "losties" and describes his technique of "water balloon evangelism," during which he would drive around in a car, randomly targeting people with balloons that contained religious tracts. Then he'd swing back with a second water balloon, and bam—his targets would be saved and baptized in the same moment!

While the clip is clearly ridiculous, I find myself wondering how different that was from my zoo experience, which ultimately reduced us to looking at people as potential targets. I can't help thinking that, when Jesus instructed his friends and followers to go and make *other* disciples, he intended them to follow his own pattern. Consider the steps Jesus followed:

- He sought those who were different from him and on the "outside" of organized religion.
- He invited them into friendship and community with him.
- He gave them a front-row seat to his life and modeled before them a life of kindness.
- He invited them to ask questions as often as they needed.
- He corrected them (sometimes gently, sometimes not) when they got it wrong.
- He experienced disappointment and even betrayal and abandonment.
- He saw past their mistakes to the people they *could* be through his grace, and therefore forgave and loved them all the same.

The reality is that Jesus' disciple-making process was at least three years long, and even then it wasn't always successful. Some like Judas, and probably many others along the way, failed to follow him, despite his personal investment in their lives. Yet, Jesus was committed to long-term relationships of love and support. It is the only pattern he ever gave us for making a disciple.

EVANGELISM REQUIRES *WORDS*

Because we are uncomfortable sharing our faith with others, we often fall back on the often-quoted dictum: "Preach the gospel at all times. If necessary, use words." We hope thereby that if we live a good life before others, then we can avoid the discomfort of faith sharing. But the opposite is true—if we're living well in relationship with others, and if they truly experience us as "good news," then we should expect them to come to us in times of need with their questions.

In those moments, it is helpful for us to remember the instructions Peter gave to early Christians: "Always be prepared to give an answer to everyone who asks you to give the reason for the hope that you have. But do this with gentleness and respect" (1 Peter 3:15 NIV). Be prepared to share your faith. Think through in advance the answer to these questions: What does it mean to follow Jesus? What difference has it made in your life? Your words don't have to be perfect or polished; they just have to be authentic and true. And whatever words we offer, we should do so with gentleness and respect. This isn't a time-share sales pitch; we don't have to pressure someone to sign on a dotted line. We simply are asked to share how the good news we live by might be good news for them as well, and then we leave the invitation open for them to respond.

EVANGELISM IS ABOUT THE *HERE AND NOW*

In the presentations of the gospel I grew up with, the speakers always closed with a question: "If you were to die tonight, where would you spend eternity?" It is a loaded question, one that presumes the sole aim of evangelism is to ensure the eternal resting place of someone's soul. I can imagine very few contexts in which someone who is seeking faith would perceive this question as caring and compassionate, rather than manipulative and off-putting.

The question that moves people more today is "What is your life about?" It has an open-ended quality; it doesn't put the dagger to anyone's throat. (But be careful that you truly listen and respond to other people's thoughts, so that you're not just asking the question so that you can tell them how you've got it all figured out!) The goal of Christian discipleship is not to give people a "ticket to heaven." The goal is to invite them to participate in God's kingdom, starting in the here and now. Start with the concerns people have for this life—the good news is relevant for today's concerns as well as helping our fears about tomorrow.

Evangelism is about our *Hearts*

The word within this chapter's title that initially gave me pause was *yearns*. My heart yearns toward many things; sharing my faith is not one of them. So I find it helpful to root evangelism within the great commandments that Jesus gave us: to love God and to love one another.

When you love people, you naturally develop wishes for them. You wish in general for them to be happy and healthy and successful. But the better you know individuals, the more specific your "yearning" for them becomes. Depending on their life situations, you might yearn for them to meet the right mates or the right group of friends, or for them to land the right jobs and find the right careers, or to have greater confidence in their own gifts and strengths. When you love people, you naturally *yearn* for them. And among the wishes you hold and hope for others, cultivate a yearning for them to know God. Ultimately, yearning for others requires us to reorient our hearts away from our own needs and desires, and to focus instead on others' joy and fulfillment.

Evangelism is *Communal* as much as *Individual*

Part of our yearning for others is a desire to *include* them in our community. We tend to think of evangelism as a "Lone Ranger" expedition; it's up to us as individuals to lead all our friends to

Christ. But the truth is, when the church fails to love its neighbors and its community, individual efforts don't carry very far. Those outside the church may think you're a nice person, but they'll also think you're the "exception" to the rule. Corporate witness will trump individual efforts any day.

On the flip side, when the church *does* love its neighbors well, the work of evangelism is so much easier. No longer is it up to a solitary individual to explain or persuade someone into the faith. Instead, we simply invite others into our community, trusting that the experience of being loved by the body of Christ will have as much transformative power as any explanations we might give of the gospel. This does not exclude the importance of individuals— personal invitation is still the most effective means of drawing someone into the church, and the greater the history of personal investment in a relationship, the more effective that invitation will be. But when we can trust that the church is a safe place to invite our friends, and we know that our congregation is just as committed to loving them as we are, then evangelism soars.

Evangelism is ultimately *God's* work

Whatever yearning we may cultivate for others, it does not even come close to the yearning that God has for them. As we pursue relationships with others, we must always invite God into the process—to help shape our hearts, to help prepare us for those moments when the door of invitation is open, to supply us with the right words and counsel, or perhaps with the sensitivity to know when to say nothing at all but to simply listen.

In his book *Just Walk Across the Room*, Bill Hybels counsels us to be available to do the work that God has given us and no more. It is not necessary in every conversation or interaction to push someone to make a faith commitment. It might be our role is simply to nudge someone toward faith, and another will come along to continue that nudging. Ultimately, we come to see the process of bringing someone to faith as not "our job" at all, but the work of God. As Paul said to the Corinthians, "I planted, Apollos watered, but God made it grow. Because of this, neither the one who plants nor the one who waters is anything, but the only one who is anything is God who makes it grow" (1 Corinthians 3:6-7).

Evangelism is *Transformative*

When I entered my first church as a young seminarian, I figured my role would be teaching other Christians how to be "better Christians." (And yes, I'm aware of how arrogant that sounds; I am not proud of my attitude, and thankfully my church loved me anyway and taught me how to be a better pastor.) But by that statement, I assumed that everyone attending would be familiar with all the same stories and traditions I knew, and my job was to enlighten them about those stories and to help them be more generous in missions and service within our community.

Then something amazing happened about six months into my time there. People within the community started responding to what we were doing, and a few families showed up on Sunday morning. At first it was children from the after-school program who brought their parents, then we started getting families from the Scouts program we housed, and soon we didn't even know where they were coming from, but new families and individuals kept coming. Many of these new visitors didn't know the stories of the Bible; they weren't familiar with our traditions or even with our "conduct codes" (children's ministry got *very* interesting). It was very chaotic and messy, but in the midst of that—the church revived.

A new energy filled our church, and it wasn't just that these new families brought youth, although that was part of it. We also recovered some part of our mission that had been forgotten, the joy of sharing Christ with those who didn't already know him, the joy of seeing individual lives (and, by extension, our surrounding community) transformed by the good news of Jesus.

It is no wonder that the largest and fastest-growing churches in our country and in our denomination have kept this mission at their core—that they exist to introduce Christ to those who are not already in a practicing relationship with God. Sharing our hope with our neighbors is the heartbeat of the church, and it remains at the center of a growing relationship with God.

THE REST OF THE STORY

Return with me to my sophomore year in high school, the Monday night after that student leadership conference. I was playing tennis with a friend of mine, Chris. He and I both played on the tennis team at school, although we were lower seeds on the team and wanted to improve our standings. We were in the same youth group as well, although it's fair to say that Chris wasn't as heavily invested. While we had the same group of friends in the youth group, Chris also moved in social circles beyond my reach—he could easily fit in with the "cool" kids who partied on the weekends, and he moved back and forth between the groups.

As always, we were having a fun and competitive match, until one of our water breaks. While we were switching sides of the court, Chris asked me about the conference I'd just attended. I told him about the "shotgun" incident, and we shared a good laugh. But then I felt this tide rising in my chest, this feeling that this is what I received all that training for, and yet I was afraid to risk our friendship and mess things up. Despite my fear, I put it out there: "Chris, has anyone ever talked to you about having a relationship with Christ?" To my surprise, Chris was open and seemed interested in continuing the conversation, so we sat down on the bench to talk.

Now I don't want to hold this up as a perfect example of evangelism; I still was operating out of an immature understanding of the gospel and a mind-set that "eternal stakes" were on the line. But there were two important differences to hold up between this moment and the zoo experience.

First off, I knew Chris and he knew me. We had a long foundation of friendship—we'd known each other since we were kids—and that friendship would've continued even if he'd blown me off. He'd seen me at my best and at my worst (for instance, he knew that I could have a "John McEnroe" temper on the court and had seen me break a few tennis rackets). In other words, I couldn't pretend to be something I wasn't. Chris could verify my words against his knowledge of my life.

Second, there was no pressure. It might've been a little tough and awkward to get into the conversation at first, but once we were talking, it was just natural. Chris could ask any questions he had; I could admit if I didn't have all the answers. The conversation was open-ended. I had no predetermined way to close the conversation and we could loop back to unresolved questions at a later time. Most important, I felt no pressure to report a result of our talk, and I was going to be Chris's friend no matter what that result would be.

Chris and I talked for almost an hour, thankfully no one else was on the tennis courts to disturb us or make us feel uncomfortable as we talked. At the end of our conversation, Chris asked me to pray with him to receive Christ. It was a simple and humble moment that I still remember to this day.

By that time, it was late, and we both had to get home. We never did finish that tennis match. But thankfully, our friendship continues to this day.

QUESTIONS

1. *What is your faith story? How would you say that following Christ has made a difference in your life?*

2. *What "thin ice" do you experience in sharing your faith with others? How does that fear affect your relationship with them?*

3. *Think about the church in which you worship. How are members encouraged to share their faith with others? How can you help your church become more outwardly focused? Are there ministries in which you can participate to help your church become more effective in reaching and welcoming its neighbors?*

4. *Are there any individuals (friends, family members) that you yearn to find a relationship with Christ? Why do you feel this yearning on their behalf?*

5. *How could sharing your faith with others deepen your own relationship with God? What would it look like to be more attentive to God's prompting to share good news with others?*

RESOURCES

Becoming a Contagious Church: Increasing Your Church's Evangelistic Temperature, by Mark Mittelberg. Grand Rapids, MI: Zondervan, 2007.

Change the World: Recovering the Message and Mission of Jesus, by Mike Slaughter. Nashville: Abingdon Press, 2010.

In the Gap: What Happens When God's People Stand Strong, by Wilfredo De Jesus. Springfield, MO: Influence Resources, 2014.

Just Walk Across the Room: Simple Steps Pointing People to Faith, by Bill Hybels. Grand Rapids, MI: Zondervan, 2006.

Outflow: Outward-Focused Living in a Self-focused World, by Steve Sjogren and David W. Ping. Loveland, CO: Group Publishing, 2007.

Unbinding the Gospel: Real Life Evangelism, by Martha Grace Reece. St. Louis: Chalice Press, 2008.

PART TWO: PROCESS

A disciple of Jesus Christ is a person who...

CHAPTER 9

Begins at One or More Points

Adolf Hansen

As people were bringing children to Jesus, he would bless them and say: "I assure you that whoever doesn't welcome God's kingdom like a child will never enter it." (Mark 10:15)

The nursery room in the church in Brooklyn, New York, was crowded that Sunday morning. Most babies were fussing, some even crying, but volunteers who cared for the infants were joyful, gentle, and kind. They seemed to exemplify the same spirit Jesus expressed when people brought children to him.

I have no recollection of that morning, but my mother described that scene to me—over and over again—as I grew up. She was so proud that, at age forty, she had borne a healthy son in a land that was foreign to her, a land where her mother and father and most of her family didn't live. She also found deep satisfaction in the love shown to her by her husband, her family (most of whom were thousands of miles away), her many friends at church, and—yes—especially God!

That Sunday morning I started my venture of becoming a disciple of Jesus Christ. And it was followed by my weekly visits to that same nursery, my subsequent baptism before I was a year old, and my times of listening to Bible stories, singing songs, and talking to God in prayer—both at church and at home—throughout my preschool years.

I began with point #4: "Shares in the life and witness of a community of disciples, including baptism and the Lord's Supper." I was too young in those early years to share in the "witness" of the community, or to participate in the "Lord's Supper," but I certainly had become a part of the community of disciples.

AT ANY ONE POINT

Individuals can begin their journey of discipleship at any of the first seven points. Some step onto the path after a direct encounter with God (#1). Others begin with a study about Jesus (#2), an identification with certain qualities of character (#3), a visit to a church (#4), a connection through a service project (#5), an experience of suffering (#6), or a concern about an afterlife (#7). Yes, persons can start at any of these points, as well as others, though they cannot lead others to become disciples (#8) until after they themselves have become disciples.

The process of becoming a disciple is sometimes gradual. Maria said, "I went to church as a baby." Don exclaimed, "I grew up in the church." Sarah put it this way, "I don't remember *not* being a disciple." In short, some begin as infants and gradually move in a variety of directions as the process unfolds. Still others begin a gradual process, but they start later in life.

For others the process begins with a sudden, or somewhat sudden, conversion experience. After finding themselves on a road leading away from God, they "repent"—*metanoeo*—the Greek word translated as "a turn around" or "an about-face."

Many of us have watched an evangelistic crusade on television.

Some of us may have attended one. We have observed those who come forward to make a decision to become disciples of Jesus Christ. They often repent and turn from their sinful ways. They ask God to forgive them and lead them in a new direction.

Gary grew up in the church; he didn't have a dramatic conversion experience. But his son went through such an experience as a young adult, after he began attending a different church. Gary then shared his concern: "My son thinks I must have a conversion experience in order to be saved. He and his pastor, as well as most people in that congregation, believe everyone needs to be converted to be a Christian. I think they're sincere, but I think they're mistaken. I already am a disciple of Jesus Christ—have been since I was a child."

The Holy Spirit works in different ways with different people. Some move through a gradual process. Others move through a conversion experience. The difficulty that emerges is that some persons think others need to go through the same type of experience as the one they had. And what complicates this even further is persons sometimes express this point of view in a judgmental manner, as Gary's son had done to his father.

Those who have experienced God's forgiveness and acceptance through a conversion experience need to respect and accept the validity of those who have come by means of a gradual process. And, likewise, those who come through a gradual process need to respect and accept the validity of those who have become disciples by means of a conversion experience. For some, this is not easy to do.

AT TWO POINTS SIMULTANEOUSLY

Oftentimes persons begin at two points at the same time. For example, they may become a part of a community of disciples and, at the same time, join with them in a service project in another town. This is what Andrew did when he decided to take a week of vacation and become a volunteer in a Habitat for Humanity project. He came because he had friends who were active in the church that was sponsoring "the build," and one of them had invited him to go with them.

Throughout the entire week Andrew listened to their words—especially during morning devotions—and observed their behavior throughout the day. What impressed him so deeply was that they really cared about the potential homeowners as well as what they were doing. During a time of debriefing on the last day Andrew spoke up: "This has been quite an experience for me. I've worked with lots of people in my remodeling business, but they're not like you. They're much more self-centered."

"We work as we do because we're trying our best to live as disciples of Jesus Christ. We sometimes fall short, but we have each other to lift us up," explained his friend from church.

"I like the way you care for others, both in your own group and those outside," said Andrew. After a few moments of quietness, his friend suggested that Andrew come to church with them next Sunday. "Yeah, I'd really like to do that," replied Andrew with a broad smile.

Sharing in the life of the community of believers and serving others in need is one combination. There are many others. They sometimes take place in the lives of adults. At other times they occur in the lives of children.

Pam was ten years old and sometimes went to church, even when her parents didn't attend. She liked being with others her own age. So when a friend invited her to come to vacation Bible school, she got permission from her mom and attended a group that met, not in a church, but in a woman's three-car garage. At a session near the end of the week she made a decision to give her life to Jesus and become his follower. Looking back as an adult, Pam said: "It was a deeply felt experience, one that became for me a very formative event. But I never told my family about it, not even my mother, because I didn't think they'd understand." Experiencing God while sharing in the life of a community of believers connects two points at the same time.

WITHOUT BEING AWARE

In some circumstances people begin the discipleship process without thinking about their point of entry. This may be what happened with those who were initially called by Jesus. Some people think Jesus walked up to Peter and Andrew, two fishermen mending their nets, and simply invited them to follow him. Others wonder if they had already heard about Jesus, had already met him in some other setting, and might even have discussed with him what it would mean if they did follow him. And then Jesus, having seen them once again, might have said, "Have you made up your minds? Are you coming with me?"

No one knows what may have preceded Jesus' invitation to follow him, but it seems likely that Peter and Andrew had given little, if any, thought to what becoming disciples might mean.

People in our lifetime may be similar. They haven't consciously thought about any particular point in becoming a disciple of Jesus Christ. They may not understand what might be involved.

Min-ji was a senior in high school. She had gone to church on Sunday mornings because her parents told her it was the thing to do. She had learned the typical Sunday school answers to questions she really wasn't asking. But she was unhappy—often depressed. She wanted to be alone most of the time and was reluctant to go to a youth group meeting. However, one Wednesday evening with nothing better to do, she went and it happened to be the night that the youth group leader was telling her personal faith story. "I carefully listened and was really moved by her experience with God," said Min-ji. "I knew I didn't have any experience like hers. I had a lot of head knowledge, but that was it."

The next week when Min-ji was in study hall, she got permission to leave the room and found herself in deep thought as she walked down the hall. Without thinking about it, she opened the door to a large, unoccupied room, and all of a sudden the bright sunlight coming through the windows flooded the darkness. "In that moment," said Min-ji, "something hit me. I sensed God's presence for the first time in my life. I felt that God really loved me; that God wanted to connect with me; that God had a purpose for my life. And in some mysterious way, it was all tied to what I could see through the windows. It was as if my altar was God's creation." This event was so powerful it changed Min-ji's life. And to this day, the outdoors is the primary place where Min-ji meets God.

Other people don't have an event they can describe. They simply have become aware of God's presence over time—sometimes a long period of time. And they have been responding to God with an ever-increasing faith. Exactly when it started is not clear, but that it did start is clear, because it's a reality! And the difficulty those persons have is that others sometimes say their faith commitment isn't real because they can't point to a specific time when they made a commitment to love God and love their neighbors as themselves. Yet those who can't pinpoint the time and place find that their relationship to God through Jesus Christ is as real as those who can name the time and place when this relationship began.

WITHOUT KNOWING WHERE OR HOW TO BEGIN

Often individuals begin without making a conscious decision about a starting point, especially when they are in their teen years.

Jason didn't attend church, but he did come to the youth group. He tried his best to play the guitar, though he only knew a few chords; however, strumming those chords gave Jason an opportunity to be part of the youth band. And then, very unexpectedly one Wednesday evening, he simply got up and walked out, right in the middle of the service. No one knew why he had left. The youth leader went outside to see if Jason was okay. To his surprise he found Jason out on the lawn, on his knees, with tears flowing down his cheeks. Neither the leader nor anyone in the group had the slightest idea that Jason would be the one turning to God that evening. Through a time of conversation and prayer, Jason asked Christ into his life.

However, that's not all. Another teenager, Barry, was in the same youth group. He had been selling drugs to Jason, as well as others at school. The youth leader knew about these activities, as well as a lot of other things going on at school. He knew Barry was under house arrest, wore an ankle bracelet, and couldn't go anywhere but to church. One night after the service was over, Barry stayed around and entered into a lengthy conversation with the youth leader and gave his heart to the Lord. "I want Jesus in my life," said Barry. "I don't want to keep living the way I have been." In the weeks that followed, Barry's life changed so noticeably that his family decided to become a part of the community of disciples where their son had found new life in Christ.

Not only are youth unclear about where or how they might begin, adults find themselves in similar uncertainty. Churches that provide a variety of ways to find God are more available to the leading of the Holy Spirit. For some people one approach might work. For others it might be a different approach. A number of people won't know where or how to begin. And sometimes those in the community of disciples won't know either. Providing an array of possibilities will likely increase the number of persons who will become disciples of Jesus Christ.

BY ASKING QUESTIONS

Many persons begin by inquiring. Yet, they keep their thoughts to themselves. Other times they verbalize what they're thinking. "When I was in college," said Jerry, "I was bombarded by some students who kept quoting four spiritual laws to me. And their attitude of haughtiness and superiority really made me angry. So I decided to study the Bible on my own so I could defend myself from those who were always quoting the same Bible verses—over and over." Jerry decided to come up with his own spiritual laws. He chose four that focused on love: God's love for me, God's love for others, my love for God, and my love for others. They became the core of his Christian life. He enjoyed sharing them with those who had tried to get him to accept theirs. He was even energized by the interactions.

Others ask questions without coming to any particular expression of faith. All they have is one question after another. And they are not helped by those they meet who only want to give answers, not engage in exploring questions. What they probably need is someone to carry on a genuine two-way conversation, not one individual asking and another individual answering the questions. The real need is listening—truly listening—and trying to understand what the questions are and what lies beneath the questions being raised.

Still other individuals think they have to have answers to their own questions—perhaps have their beliefs all worked out—before they can become disciples of Jesus Christ. They don't realize Jesus simply invited people to "come and see" (John 1:39). That is, begin the journey without being certain where it is going to lead.

Jesus met people where they were. And so it is today: "God" (or "the risen Christ" or "the Holy Spirit") meets people where they are and invites them "to love God with all their heart, soul, mind, and strength" or "to receive Jesus Christ as their Savior and Lord" or "to surrender their lives to the Holy Spirit." The language is different in each of these descriptions, but the experience is basically the same.

Before the beginning

Individuals sometimes have a beginning that precedes what they think is the beginning. They naturally rely on the understanding they have, yet that awareness may, at times, be somewhat limited.

For example, when does the birth of a child begin? Is it when an egg and a sperm unite? Is it when a pregnancy is confirmed? Is it when delivery occurs? Or did the birth process begin when the couple decided to have a baby? In any case, it's not a singular event. It's part of a process.

Jesus spoke with Nicodemus and said, "Unless someone is born anew [born from above], it's not possible to see God's kingdom" (John 3:3). He also said, "Unless someone is born of water and the Spirit, it's not possible to enter God's kingdom" (John 3:5). In these verses, was Jesus' reference to a moment in time or to a process that goes beyond just a moment?

It's interesting that this is the only time that Jesus speaks about new birth in any of the Gospels. In other words, it's a rare rather than a common expression of Jesus. Yes, similar wording does show up in some epistles, but even there it is not wording that is commonplace.

In our day, if someone makes a decision for Christ—either in a conversion experience, or a confirmation experience—is it a moment in time, or part of a process? Is it just a decision, or is it a decision that results in a changed life?

John Wesley was aware of beginnings that preceded a beginning.

He called it "prevenient grace." By that he meant God is present in people's lives even before they are consciously aware of it. That is, God's grace is active in awakening a desire for God, strengthening that awakening, and graciously leading persons in the direction of finding a relationship with God. In other words, God's activity has been there all along, as persons are being called to respond to God's initiative.

Beginning again

Persons sometimes begin, and stop, and begin again. And they do it in many different ways. For example, Betty was raised in the church and gradually became a disciple of Jesus Christ, or so she thought. However, in her teenage years she realized her real interest was in being with her friends and going on mission trips, not following Jesus. In her college years she got away from church altogether—a trend that often emerges at that age. She started drinking heavily. After graduation she lived alone and became increasingly dependent on alcohol. She decided to accept a part-time job so she could begin law school, but just kept on drinking—at times uncontrollably. Eventually she graduated and fell in love with a man who was not a religious person. She married, but continued her heavy drinking. As years went by, her career and her marriage were increasingly threatened by her alcoholism. Yet, she couldn't stop. She kept on saying, "I want the freedom to drink as much as I want."

Betty saw her life falling apart. She even had to give up her career. Finally, at her wits' end, she sought help by going to a stress center at a local hospital. She acknowledged her need and began taking steps to change. As she worked with a counselor week after week, and month after month, childhood memories of church school classes brought back some of what she had learned about

Jesus. She became increasingly drawn to him in ways she didn't understand. And then, she returned to church, and for the first time in her life she decided to become a true disciple of Jesus Christ. Over time, her marriage was repaired, her alcohol dependence ended, and she began to flourish in her newfound faith: "I grew in my realization that I needed to follow what God wanted, not what I wanted, to find fulfillment in life."

Other individuals have followed a more checkered pattern. As Connie put it, "I went to church. Dropped out. Went to another church for a while. Dropped out. Went to still another church. Dropped out"—a pattern that seemed like it was never going to stop. "Finally," she said, "I went to one more church on a Sunday morning, sat in the back row, and listened to this incredible choir singing the anthem. I was so moved by what I heard. I felt God speaking to me—so clearly and so powerfully. For the first time in my life I got in touch with God. And now, years later, I'm still at that church; I'm singing in the choir; and I'm finally living my life as a real disciple of Jesus Christ."

The opportunity to begin again is always possible in the process of becoming a disciple of Jesus Christ—regardless of the circumstances in which persons find themselves.

CHAPTER 10

Continues to Other Points

Adolf Hansen

"I'm sure about this: the one who started a good work in you
will stay with you to complete the job by the day of Christ Jesus."
(Philippians 1:6)

The sanctuary in the church in Brooklyn, New York, was filled
with children and youth, as well as many parents and other adults.
It had been a festive atmosphere for the entire day—a Saturday
filled with games, music, drama, food, and stories.

It was late in the afternoon that we had our closing service of
worship. We sang songs, heard a Bible story, and listened to a very
caring woman share that Jesus wanted to come into our lives. She
led us in singing the song: "Into my heart, into my heart, come into
my heart, Lord Jesus. Come in today. Come in to stay. Come into
my heart, Lord Jesus."[1] She then invited those of us who wanted to
invite Jesus into our hearts to come forward. It made enough sense
to me—even though I was only six years old—and I responded, as
did a number of others. We were led in a unison prayer and then
we returned to our seats. It was not a very emotional experience. It
was, however, my opportunity to invite Jesus into my life.

A couple of years later I received my own Bible and, at the

encouragement of my mother, I printed these words on the opening page: "When I was six years old I gave my heart to Jesus." (And now, many years later, I still have the top part of that page.) I took a keen interest in learning about Jesus, at home and at church. I had begun with point #4, "Shares in the life and witness of a community of believers," but had continued to point #2, "Follows the life and teachings of Jesus."

I experienced considerable growth in understanding the meaning of this initial decision to become a follower of Jesus. For example, when I entered junior high school and studied the human heart in my first biology class, I remembered that I had invited Jesus into my heart when I was six years old. I amused myself by wondering if I had invited Jesus into my right auricle or my left ventricle, though I was too embarrassed to breathe a word about this to anyone, especially my friends. I knew, of course, that such concrete thinking had been okay at age six, but was no longer a way to express my faith. I changed my terminology over a period of time and learned to speak of a relationship with Jesus Christ, one that was so close that it seemed—at times—he was living "within" me. Little did I know that the Apostle Paul had written about being "in Christ" and having "Christ . . . in you" (Colossians 1:27).

Beginning with #4, and continuing to #2, did not put an end to my venture. Instead, it opened up other possibilities. During my high school and college years I was able to grasp more fully—in my heart as well as my head—the forgiveness and acceptance of God (#1), as well as what it meant to anticipate a future life in the presence of God (#7). Following graduation from college, I married a very gracious woman and learned more fully what the fruit of the Spirit looked like (#3). I attended seminary and, through my field education experiences, I became involved with one form of service after another (#5). Through my early years as a pastor, I developed a passion for leading others to become disciples of Jesus Christ (#8). And, throughout my lifetime, I have been led to participate in God's suffering and transformation in many situations (#6), starting with my upbringing in New York City and continuing in a variety of places in this country and abroad.

You may also have been engaged in all eight of these points, though it is likely that you didn't move in the same manner as I did. Or, you may have experienced some, but not all. Or, you may have experienced only one or two, or none at all.

FROM ONE POINT TO ANOTHER

People continue the process of becoming disciples by moving from an initial starting point to one or more other points. As there is no particular point at which an individual must begin, so there is no particular point to which an individual must move.

Todd had been a member of his suburban church for several years. He missed many Sundays, but came often enough that he was acquainted with a number of fellow worshipers. He attended church because he had learned to do that with his parents when he was a child and now, as an adult, he thought it was somewhat important.

However, Todd was in a searching mode. He had connections with other people when he came to worship but never had what he called "a real connection with God." And then, one Sunday morning, it happened! He wasn't expecting it; he wasn't even sure what he was looking for. But as he sat there during the sermon, though not listening very closely, Todd found himself sensing God's presence in a profound way: "It was something I had never experienced before. I just felt, for the very first time, that I was accepted by God, not because I deserved it, but because God was showering grace on me—just the way I was." He went on to describe his experience by saying, "I felt a profound sense of forgiveness and inner peace that I had never known before."

When Todd saw his pastor after the service was over, he told him about his experience. His pastor listened very carefully, invited him into his office, took a volume off his shelf, and read the following words from John Wesley: "In the evening, I went very unwillingly to a society in Aldersgate Street, where one was reading Luther's Preface to the Epistle to the Romans. About a quarter before nine, while he was describing the change which God works in the heart through faith in Christ, I felt my heart strangely warmed. I felt I did trust in Christ, Christ alone for salvation, and an assurance was given me that he had taken away *my* sins, even mine, and saved me from the law of sin and death."[2]

Todd bowed his head, paused, and then indicated that he hadn't heard that story before. But then he added, "How interesting! I guess my heart was 'strangely warmed' too, though I wouldn't have been able to describe my experience in such eloquent words."

Todd had moved from his starting point, "sharing in the life of the community of believers," to "experiencing the forgiveness and acceptance of God."

Emily, on the other hand, grew up in a small rural town. Her parents took her to church on a regular basis; she attended because she had no choice in the matter. When she was twelve, her mother's insistence that she attend revival services particularly frustrated her, especially when she had to attend services at a number of other churches in the county where she lived. And she knew—deep down—that her mother wanted her to go forward when the altar call was given so she would be "saved."

Finally one evening, she decided to go forward while the congregation was singing the familiar hymn, "Softly and Tenderly Jesus Is Calling." She wasn't sure if she was doing it for her mother's sake, or if she really meant it, but she did go. She remembers what an emotionally filled experience it was. The preacher was loud, so was the singing, and so were those who gathered around her at the altar rail. But she did make a decision to accept Christ as her Savior and Lord. "I didn't really understand what my decision meant, but I realized that my decision was probably just a beginning and that I had a lot more to learn."

Emily had moved from her starting point, "sharing in the life of a community of believers," to another point, "experiencing the forgiveness and acceptance of God"—just as Todd had done, though in a very different manner.

TO ANY POINT THEREAFTER

Persons keep on growing by moving to any and all of the remaining points. They can begin at any one, progress to any other, and then advance to still others.

After worship one Sunday, Jane, the pastor of an urban church, noticed a man in the hallway, reading the bulletin board just inside the main entrance. She approached him and asked, "What's going on?" It was then that he took a deep breath, looked at Jane as tears started to roll down his cheeks. He paused, composed himself enough to talk, and then told her his name was Charlie. He indicated he lived in the area and often passed by the church as he walked to his office, but had never considered coming inside. They continued to talk and walked down the hall to Jane's office where they talked some more.

When Charlie had been arrested the night before on a charge of DUI, he was terrified. Even though he had been released that morning, he realized his license could be revoked. He then thought of other consequences, including losing his job, because his work required that he do a fair amount of driving. He also admitted he had a drinking problem that had contributed to his divorce and had impacted all of his relationships. He had felt so alone that morning that he had simply walked into the church.

Over the next several months, Charlie had more conversations with Jane. He did lose his license for a time, but not his employment. He attended Alcoholics Anonymous meetings, entered the twelve-step program, learned that acceptance was the release of all hope for a better past, and stopped drinking. At the same time he attended worship on a regular basis, became involved in a variety of activities at the church, connected at deep levels to others in this community of disciples, and eventually became a trustee. But most important, he was led through these activities, and through these relationships, to become a disciple of Jesus Christ!

TOWARD PERFECTION

Individuals advance to other points, until they reach a greater and greater degree of maturity. In The United Methodist Church, this is called "Christian perfection" or "perfect love." It comes from verses such as Matthew 5:48 in which Jesus says, "Be perfect, therefore, as your heavenly Father is perfect" (NRSV).

In the paragraph preceding this verse Jesus is reminding his listeners that they had heard the teaching that neighbors should be loved and enemies hated. But he now declares to them that enemies as well as neighbors should be loved. In short, he is broadening the scope of love by using the verb, *teleioo,* often translated as "perfect," though the root meaning of the verb is "to make complete" or "to make mature." In the Common English Bible, the verse reads: "Therefore, just as your heavenly Father is complete in showing love to everyone, so also you must be complete."

This verb is also used in James 1:4, where the writer exhorts his readers by saying: "that you may be fully mature, complete, and lacking in nothing." In other words, to exemplify "perfect love," enemies as well as neighbors must be included. This is what Wesley meant when he wrote *A Plain Account of Christian Perfection*.[3] He defined Christian perfection as loving God with all of one's heart, mind, soul, and strength. It is also what United Methodists mean today when speaking about "going on to perfection."

FROM ONE LEVEL TO ANOTHER

Individuals usually begin at a level that grows out of their own life situations. This varies with each person. For one it may be an awakening to a deeper level of meaning. For another it may be an awakening to a deeper level of relationship.

Luis, a fourteen-year-old member of a youth group, had several meaningful times during his yearlong confirmation class. It culminated with a retreat during which the group studied Colossians 3, especially the thought of dying to sin and being raised to new life. In closing they participated in a "remember your baptism" service. Each youth was given a small, hand-carved wooden cross, and—one by one—they dipped their crosses into the water at the edge of the lake. Then they met in small groups and discussed what they had done and what it meant. It was a powerful experience for Luis, who had never done this before.

At a subsequent youth meeting, small groups met to debrief the retreat. Luis remembered the discussion about sin at the retreat and spoke up. "I think I've come up with a new way of understanding sin," he said. "For me, it's an obstacle, something that's bigger than God."

"What do you mean?" asked the youth leader.

"When we make something bigger than God, we sin," replied Luis. "We're ashamed. We don't go to God to talk about it." A deeper level of understanding. Adam and Eve all over again.

Sometimes a deeper level in relationship emerges. When Anne and Kyle were in their mid-thirties, they wanted to make their discipleship journey more meaningful. They'd been attending a large church almost every Sunday for nearly four years, but didn't feel close to anyone. So they decided they would do something about it. With the assistance of a staff member, they put an announcement in the bulletin that invited persons to come to a new group, "Busy Couples Book Study." They wanted to learn; they wanted to get to know others like themselves; and they wanted to have fun doing it. To their surprise, six couples expressed interest. They met one time, discussed ideas, and decided to meet once a month.

The group came together—all fourteen of them—the next month, and each month thereafter (with schedule conflicts, of course, on occasion) for the next three years. For the first time in their lives, Anne and Kyle were able to connect at a deep level with others who bought into the same values: serious study, meaningful relationships, and lots of fun. And the interesting thing to them was that none of the persons in the group were their friends before they started. Anne summarized her insight well when she said, "I didn't really know I needed that relationship piece until it happened. It made coming to church much more meaningful."

Though Not Always Forward

People proceed from one point to another, yet the movement may at times be backward rather than forward. This is common for most individuals. It is especially common for youth during their formative adolescent years.

Joe was the director of a youth program in a vibrant congregation. He and his colleagues at church developed a confirmation program that started in the fall, continued throughout the school year, and concluded with a Sunday morning commitment service before the entire congregation.

Components of the program included structured times of engagement between students and parents (or primary-care givers), students and their individual mentors, as well as students and individual youth leaders. Each of these relationships developed in similar ways, though each was somewhat different. For the youth leaders it meant an individual meeting with a select number of students once each month for eight meetings.

Joe met with Scott at McDonald's each month. Scott would walk there from school, and Joe would drive him home. They talked at length each time they met, and the conversations led them deeper and deeper into an understanding of what it meant to be a disciple of Jesus Christ. And, as is common with early adolescents, their conversation led them sometimes to talk about steps going forward, or steps going backward, or steps going in all sorts of directions.

During one of these meetings they were sitting across from the large TV screen, listening to a sports commentator talk about an athlete who had made a poor choice, when Scott commented to Joe: "He's going to need our prayers. He really made a bad choice. This is going to impact not only him, but his family." This was a moment of insight for Scott. He was connecting the dots. He was taking a step forward, a very important one, because last month he had shared with Joe how he himself had made a bad choice, had taken a step backward.

THOUGH NOT ALWAYS IN A STRAIGHT LINE

Persons move in ways that include curves or ups and downs, unexpected pitfalls or surprising times of joy and celebration. That's how life is, though the dynamics of one individual's life never replicates another.

Kathy and Amy had traveled together in six different European countries during their semester abroad. Now they were seniors in college and were dreaming of taking one more trip together right after graduation. But as they talked, it became clear that would not be possible. They simply didn't have enough money!

During their spring break, they went to see *The Way*, a film that portrays the Camino de Santiago, a pilgrimage route to the shrine of the Apostle St. James, the cathedral in Galicia, Spain. And they were so excited when they walked out of the theater that night that they decided this was the location for their next trip—someday when they could travel to Europe once again.

The discussion after the movie soon turned to the symbolism of the film. It seemed to parallel the pilgrimage of becoming a disciple of Jesus Christ. They would talk about a scene in the movie, and then relate it to their own lives. "That's just like me when I go from one place to the next," said Kathy.

"I know what you mean," added Amy.

"Right now I can't wait to see what job I'm going to get. I'm hoping it's something I'll really like," answered Kathy. "I guess I'm going to have to trust God to lead me."

The conversation went on and on as they discussed scenes from the movie, and then connected them to their lives—right now and in the years to come. They admitted they didn't know what pitfalls might lie ahead, but felt that was okay, maybe even desirable. "The challenging times will certainly come," said Amy, "but let's keep on looking forward to the good times. We know they'll come too. We'll make sure of that!"

THOUGH NOT ALWAYS EASY

People try to move ahead on their journey, yet sometimes find it's difficult. The place from which a person begins is crucial. It can be a relatively easy path to discipleship, or an incredibly difficult one.

When a girl grows up in an abusive home, where negative words are spoken, hostile attitudes expressed, and unbelievably cruel actions take place, she cannot begin to comprehend a God of steadfast love. She has not experienced anything like that—not even close to that. Therefore, finding a way to experience the eight points described in this volume is next to impossible until other non-abusive persons find ways to enter such an environment or individuals find a path out of that situation on their own initiative.

When an African American youth grows up and learns his great-great-great-grandfather was a slave, he struggles to grasp what life was like at that time and every time since then. He wonders why people in that day, and even this day, could be so blind to injustices carried out in all sorts of ways. He wrestles with the impact his background has had on his life, his family, and his world. He looks at ways injustices are still carried out today, especially through structures that in many instances favor those who are in power—economically, socially, and politically. As a result, it is often more difficult for persons with backgrounds that have barriers ingrained in their cultural history to experience the points inherent in the definition of a disciple of Jesus Christ.

When a boy or a man realizes he is attracted to other men rather than women, and when a girl or woman realizes she is attracted to other women rather than men, they often become aware of difficulty in expressing who they really are—at home, at school, at church, and at work. Although they can experience all the points identified in the definition of a disciple—just like anyone else— they learn that the path is sometimes more complex for them, particularly when others don't understand them or don't accept them for who they are. Furthermore, others sometimes judge them in ways that are contrary to the qualities of true disciples of Jesus Christ. And those persons who are bisexual or transgender often encounter additional complexities.

Experiencing the eight points of definition in this book is more difficult for some than for others. That awareness is not only important to grasp, it is also a call to those who experience less difficulty to reject any notion that they are somehow better because they find the venture easier. It is a call to find ways to walk alongside those who are having more difficulty and to share life with them as much as is possible and reasonable.

Notes

1. "Into My Heart," by Harry D. Clarke, *The Faith We Sing* (Nashville: Abingdon Press, 2000), 2160, stanza 1. Copyright Hope Publishing Co.

2. John Wesley, *The Journal of John Wesley*, vol. 18, edited by Reginald Ward and Richard P. Heitzenrater (Nashville: Abingdon Press, 1988), 249-50.

3. John Wesley, *The Works of John Wesley*, vol. 13, ed. Paul Wesley Chilcote and Kenneth I. Collins (Nashville: Abingdon Press, 2013).

CHAPTER 11

Engages with Points in Unique Ways

Adolf Hansen

"God is the one who enables you both to want and to actually live out his good purposes." (Philippians 2:13)

The decades I've lived in New York, Connecticut, Illinois, and Indiana have enabled me to connect with a wide array of people. The visits I've made to numerous countries abroad have further broadened and deepened my connections.

The theological perspectives I've encountered have ranged from the far right to the far left, with considerable time spent with others whom I would place at various points between these extremes, whether they are Protestant (evangelical, moderate, or progressive), Roman Catholic, or Orthodox; whether they are Western (particularly Jewish) or Eastern; whether they are agnostics, atheists, or simply "none of the above." Life as a professor and administrator in university and graduate school environments, as well as a pastor in local congregations, has made this possible. And for me, it has been fascinating!

I've learned so much from so many! Experiences with the divine in various ethnic and cultural settings have opened my eyes to diverse ways in which God encounters human beings. Social settings have helped me understand people with different as well as similar lifestyles. Conceptual formulations about life by those who hold a range of viewpoints different from my own have assisted me in comprehending a panorama of perspectives.

INDIVIDUAL DETERMINANTS

People are unique. They approach the process of becoming disciples of Jesus Christ out of their own situations. And within those situations there are numerous determinants. Some of them are **personal**. One is age: whether a person is a child, a youth, an emerging adult, an adult of some years, or a senior citizen. A second is gender, with all of the implications inherent in being a woman or a man. A third is sexual orientation, whether heterosexual or homosexual—lesbian, gay, bisexual, or transgender. A fourth is the variety of personality types and how each type experiences life.

Other determinants can be identified within the **cultural context** in which individuals find themselves. One of these is nationality, including languages persons speak and practices they carry out. Another is race, both personal identities and primary communities—a more and more complicated designation since there is an increasing awareness of multicultural identifications.

Still other determinants grow out of a person's **experience**, beginning with family upbringing. If parents (or primary caregivers) have admirable qualities of character, and demonstrate them in gracious and loving ways, children will likely have positive influences in their lives—the kind that will enable them to have positive role models for their behavior. On the other hand, if one or both parents are abusive—emotionally, verbally, physically, and/or sexually—children will find it difficult to think of God as other than one who is like their father or mother.

Beyond the immediate family, there are numerous **relationships** that individuals have developed in the past—both positive and negative—as well as in the present. These often include relationships with other family members, friends, acquaintances, colleagues in school, work, or the community, and most important for some persons, relationships with people at church.

Underlying a number of these determinants are the **beliefs and values** a person holds regarding God, Jesus Christ, the Holy Spirit, the Bible, the church, and other theological tenets. And not only these but also the beliefs and values a person affirms regarding all of life, especially issues pertaining to personal ethics and social justice.

It is not difficult to affirm that all persons are unique in what they bring to the process of becoming disciples of Jesus Christ. At the same time, it is difficult to grasp the life situations out of which that process has emerged when individuals are not like us. It will necessitate careful and prolonged discernment to comprehend the journeys of others and to avoid using our own journeys to render judgments about their journeys.

NETWORKS WITH OTHERS

Individuals were not created to live in isolation. They were made to live in a range of connections, starting with the family—however that is defined—and continuing with many others throughout life.

Ways in which networks impact the process of discipleship vary. However, one dimension that has shown itself to be highly influential is the manner in which mentoring takes place. In my life, mentoring is what I received first from my parents, and then from family members, friends, leaders at church, teachers in school, peer relationships, professors in college, seminary, graduate school, and, of course, students. It is also what I presently receive from those with whom I associate most fully: my spouse, my family, colleagues in my work, and social acquaintances in a variety of settings.

Mentoring initially came from others to me; but that changed over the years, particularly in my career in university and seminary teaching and administration. I became a mentor to others, especially my students—thousands of them. I felt it was such a privilege. However, I soon realized that they were also mentoring me. And, as time went on, I specifically asked them to mentor me. To some this came as a surprise; but when they realized they had many things they could teach me, relationships emerged that at times were profound. It became a process of **mutual mentoring**. And through decades of such relationships, I've come to realize that two-way mentoring is by far the most significant way of learning, not only in general terms, but also the most significant way of becoming a disciple of Jesus Christ.

In addition to mutual mentoring, however, I also learned the incredible value of **reverse mentoring**. When I read Earl Creps's book *Reverse Mentoring: How Young Leaders Can Transform the Church and Why We Should Let Them*,[1] I became aware of two words that described what I had been doing for years.

The development of my experience of reverse mentoring came to the forefront in my years as a professor at the University of Indianapolis (1971–82). Particularly important was my desire to understand life more fully from the perspective of women. I team-taught a class with Christina, a highly regarded feminist, and asked her if she would be my mentor in the way I considered women— the words I spoke, the images I used, the assumptions I made, and so forth. It was at times an eye-opener for me. She invited me to do the same from my perspective as a man. We both learned, but I'm certain I did most of the learning! And through that team teaching we became very close colleagues for years thereafter. As a result of that learning—and similar learning since—I consider myself a "repentant sexist." By this I mean I have diligently tried to understand women's issues; I have grown a lot, but I still have more to learn.

The second development of my reverse mentoring became more prominent in my years as an administrator and professor at Garrett-Evangelical Theological Seminary (1983–2003). What became especially important to me in those years was my desire to understand life as fully as possible from the perspective of persons with ethnicity other than my own: African American, Latin American, Native American, and Asian.

The most meaningful connection I made was with Vanessa, an African American woman who was a graduate student at both the seminary and Northwestern University. What turned out to be a significant friendship began with times of conflict between her views and those expressed in policies of the seminary. Numerous conversations took place, some that were rather heated, but the mind-boggling candor and the heartfelt sharing over many months led us to understand, respect, and trust each other at ever-increasing depths. When I, as a vice president of the institution, asked her to be my ongoing mentor as it pertained to words I spoke, images I used, and assumptions I made regarding African Americans, she smiled and said, "Really?" And I said, "Yes. Let's try it." To which she said, "Okay." And then I added, "But when you have something to say to me, tell me in private. Okay?" She agreed.

In the months and years that followed we had conversations—whether planned or on the spur of the moment, whether in my office or in a hallway—that focused within the context of learning. As a result of those conversations—and other conversations since—I consider myself a "repentant racist." I have grown a lot; but I'm not done learning, especially when it comes to the relationship between race and power, subculture and dominant culture, individual racism and institutionalized racism.

To this day I am still learning from mentors, still becoming—hopefully—a more fruitful disciple of Jesus Christ. I currently have numerous reverse mentors in a wide range of situations in life, including my colleagues with whom I've written this book.

AT PARTICULAR OCCASIONS IN LIFE

Persons may experience some of the eight points defined in this book at special times in their lives. They may take place during a time when a passage—a stage of life—is happening, whether it is in the life of the church or outside.

One of these passages may take place when a person is baptized, either as a child or as an adult. If it occurs soon after birth, the occasion is more important for the parents, other members of the family, and those present in the congregation on the day of the baptism. If later in life, either at the time of confirmation, or the time of joining the church, the occasion is more significant for the person being baptized.

Another passage may occur at the time of confirmation, especially if sufficient instruction precedes this event, so that the one being confirmed remembers her or his baptism, grasps the connection between baptism and confirmation, and makes an intentional decision to become a disciple of Jesus Christ. To confirm one's faith, begun many years before, is an essential component of the act of confirmation. However, for those who may not have a faith to confirm, the time of confirmation becomes an occasion for making a public commitment to receive Jesus Christ as Savior and Lord.

Still another passage is the time a person joins the church—the community of disciples—particularly if a person is joining by profession of faith. However, when individuals transfer membership from another congregation, they can still renew the commitment made when they became members of the church for the first time.

Of course individuals may begin the process of becoming a disciple of Jesus Christ at other times—as described in various parts of this book, as well as those not mentioned in this volume. And at each of these times, as well as in other seasons in life, individuals can also move away from these points and later return, or move away and never return.

AT TIMES OF CRISIS

Individuals often engage one or more of these points when a crisis is about to happen, when it actually takes place, or after it has occurred. And for the person who is a disciple of Jesus Christ, the words of Romans 8:28 can be a source of encouragement and strength: "God works for good in everything" (personal translation).

Steve experienced a series of crises throughout his sixty-nine years, and worked through each of them with the awareness that God was always with him, and was always active in bringing good out of his struggles.

An early struggle took place when he was drafted into the Army after his second year in college. He knew relatively little about the Vietnam War when he left home, but learned during his first week in Vietnam that he would be dealing with matters of life and death on a daily basis. By the end of that horrendous week, he had faced death so dramatically that he said to himself: "I don't think I'll be able to really live, if I don't accept death." From the moment he drew that conclusion, he really did live in a courageous way. He was no longer afraid of death!

Years later, at age forty-six, after completing a few mini-marathons without improving his time, he went to the doctor for a checkup and learned that two arteries were blocked, one at 98 percent and the other at 99 percent. Bypass heart surgery took place almost immediately, and healing ensued as expected. But it was the profound spiritual impact that the experience had in his life that led him to read the Bible from cover to cover, to take courses in understanding the life and teachings of Jesus more fully, and to enter into various forms of ministry in the hospital, in prison, in church, and in his own home.

Then, at the age of sixty-two, Steve had to have a stent inserted in his heart. The procedure unexpectedly popped an artery. He went into cardiopulmonary arrest and came very close, once again, to dying. When he was brought back to consciousness he said, "I'd better get busy serving the Lord. I may not have much time left." And that's what he has been doing ever since!

Many others have responded in extraordinary ways as they have dealt with serious illness. Jenny struggled for years with melanoma and its effects on her body—surgery, skin grafts, and treatments of all sorts. And, in the midst of all these crises, she smiled in a very genuine manner and said, "I thank God for every day."

Benjamin was diagnosed with such a severe case of lymphoma that he was hospitalized for thirty days of intensive treatment, and was given only a fifty-fifty chance to live. He prayed every waking minute during those days, put his complete trust in God, was released, gained strength, became active once again at church, and declared: "I want to serve God in every way I can."

Many others are also noteworthy in the way they have dealt with the death of a parent, a spouse, a sibling, or a child. They have expressed faith in the midst of deep-felt anguish. Kayla did this when she lost her husband. Richard did this when his son took his own life. Carlos did this when his wife died.

Still others are remarkable in their expressions of faith, as they have worked through family issues. Rosemary was deeply hurt when she learned her husband of six years had an affair with another woman who became pregnant with his child, but Rosemary never gave up her faith though she did divorce her husband.

Craig was alienated from his parents as well as some of his siblings, when he let them know he is gay, but he continued to affirm and deepen his faith as a disciple of Jesus Christ. He had to keep reminding them, as well as others, that he was a person of sacred worth just as they were, even though his sexual orientation was different.

I have also experienced a deepening of my own faith in my times of crisis: first, when one of our daughters underwent nine major surgeries during her teenage years due to a growth in her midbrain, and on two occasions, almost died; and second, when our other daughter, in her adult years, was killed when she was struck by a vehicle. I've written a narrative dealing with these circumstances and included it in the postscript of my book *Three Simple Truths: Experiencing Them in Our Lives*.[2]

To Varying Degrees

People can experience any and all of these points in a limited manner or to a substantial extent. They can do this in a group or by themselves.

One day Jesus and his disciples came to a town named Bethsaida. People brought a blind man to Jesus for healing. Using his own saliva, Jesus put his hands on the man's eyes, and then asked if he could see anything. The man said, "I see people. They look like trees, only they are walking around." Then Jesus put his hands on the man's eyes again and this time his sight was fully restored. He saw everything clearly (Mark 8:22-26).

In the paragraph preceding this story Jesus expresses his concern that the disciples do not understand very well what he is doing and teaching. In the paragraph that follows, Jesus asks his disciples who they think he really is. And the story of the blind man comes between these two conversations. It is Mark's way of portraying the disciples in the process of learning. They see, but only in part; they need to see more fully.

How similar this is to people becoming disciples in our lifetime: understanding in part, and then more fully. This variation in degree takes place over time, both within an individual as well as among individuals. In short, persons mature in their experience of the points enumerated in the first eight chapters of this book, yet they do it at different rates and in different ways.

Awareness in becoming a disciple emerges over time. For some it begins early in life. For others it begins later in life—at forty, fifty, sixty, or beyond. But whenever the journey begins, people can move toward maturity in their own way. They can, for example, learn about the life of Jesus and his teachings at any age, at any pace, and to any degree of depth they choose.

Sometimes those in the community of disciples become an integral part of the process. In one congregation, a group of women decided to form what they called a "spiritual formation group." After a year of intentional study and practice of spiritual disciplines, four of them continued as a "covenant group," not only for their own growth but also for the growth of others. They took steps to learn about the needs of others in the congregation, regularly met and prayed for these individuals, and then wrote a personal note to each of them. One member of the group, Shirley, shared with me her spiritual booklet of forty-four pages of names and addresses, twenty per page, for a total of 880 individuals contacted in the last six years. She explained, "This booklet is mine, but I'm only one of the women. Three others have their own booklets with even a larger number of names."

I responded by saying, "That means there are between 3,500 and 4,000 individuals who have received prayer, followed by a note of encouragement and support during the past six years." All I could say to myself was, "Wow!" The women make the cards, buy the envelopes, and pay for the postage. And, even more significant, they never broadcast what they are doing. They simply pray and send notes when they learn about needs, and they do it as their response to the leading of the Holy Spirit.

In some or all of the ways

Some persons experience only a few of the eight points. Others share in an ongoing dynamic process that leads them to engage in most or even all of the points. And whenever this process—however limited or extensive—is an involvement of the head and the heart, the fullness of discipleship emerges in significant and powerful ways!

The potential for engaging with all eight points is higher for some individuals than others. Those who share in the life of a community of believers that exemplify all of the points have more opportunity to experience them. Whereas those congregations that focus primarily on a select number of the points are less likely to do so.

Furthermore, those individuals who have lived in the same geographical location most or all of their lives will likely have been exposed to a more limited expression of these points than those who have visited or moved to a variety of places. In addition, those who have maintained their participation in one denominational context without participation in events beyond the life of their own congregation may have more limited possibilities for engaging in all of the eight points. In like fashion, persons who have not participated in ecumenical or interfaith activities outside the life of their own tradition may also have more limited opportunities to understand perspectives outside of their own.

On occasion individuals have vocational opportunities that enable them to be exposed to many or even all of the eight points through a series of employment positions. Phil was such an individual. He served on the staff of congregations in seven different judicatories: Christian Church (Disciples of Christ), Christian Church (Independent), Evangelical Lutheran Church in America, Lutheran Church-Missouri Synod, American Baptist Churches (USA), Presbyterian Church (USA), and The United Methodist Church. These opportunities enriched both his understanding and his experience.

In whatever ways individuals engage with these eight points, this venture is not carried out on the assumption that human beings can experience some or all of these points in their own strength. No! Authentic experience of discipleship can only take place when human beings acknowledge and participate in the affirmation of the Apostle Paul: "God is the one who enables you both to want and to actually live out his good purposes" (Philippians 2:13). It is God at work throughout this venture that makes it not only possible but also incredibly meaningful and powerful!

NOTES

1. Earl Creps, *Reverse Mentoring: How Young Leaders Can Transform the Church and Why We Should Let Them* (San Francisco: Jossey-Bass, 2008).
2. Adolf Hansen, *Three Simple Truths: Experiencing Them in Our Lives* (Portland, OR: Inkwater Press, 2014).

CHAPTER 12

Develops Through a Lifelong Process

Adolf Hansen and Colleagues

"The message of the cross... is the power of God for those of us who are being saved." (1 Corinthians 1:18)

We have not completed our journey in becoming disciples of Jesus Christ. When Paul wrote the passage cited above (as well as 1 Corinthians 15:2), he spoke about individuals who are in the process of "being saved," a verb in the present tense that signifies ongoing action. Other ways to translate this verb from the original Greek is being "healed" or "made whole." Whatever words we may use, the process has a beginning, a continuation, and an ending.

Each of us who has written the foregoing chapters has come to the realization that "being saved"—becoming a disciple of Jesus Christ—is a lifelong venture. Yet we have come to that understanding at different times in our lives, and in various ways. What follows is a personal word of witness from each of us.

BRENT WRIGHT (CHAPTER 1)

I have always been a rule guy. I like the clarity of specific boundaries and the comfort of knowing that I'm doing things right. I tend to see things in binary ways—black or white, on or off, right or wrong, in or out.

I saw the Bible through this lens. What are the rules? What's the moral of that story? My goal was to figure it out, to boil it down to the right answer.

I understood Christian life through this lens for a long time too. Salvation was a finish line, and the goal was to cross the line. The rest of life, after getting saved, was about avoiding backsliding. Being saved was a simple matter of in or out.

When I began to learn scripture in a deeper way, I began to hear God saying something new through the same passages I thought I had already figured out. I began to realize that God's truth is bigger than my answers. God's truth has more in common with a portrait in a million shades of gray than a canvas with halves painted black and white. Learning to see scripture in all its shades of gray showed me that discipleship isn't in-or-out; it's a lifelong journey.

JILL MOFFETT HOWARD (CHAPTER 2)

My first realization that discipleship is a lifelong journey occurred soon after I began seeking Jesus as Savior and Lord. When my path to Christianity began, I had many questions, but not many answers. I wanted a quick fix. I wanted something that would assure me that I was, in fact, on the correct path. However, it took me awhile to realize that there is no "correct" path to follow. We each have our own journey to discover the heart of faith. We walk our own path, but we follow the same Lord.

With this realization, I began to understand that moments of doubt and questions are key moments on the lifelong journey of discipleship. If I had never questioned, then I wouldn't be where I am in my life of faith today. If I had never doubted, then I wouldn't be able to fully celebrate the moments of clarity about my faith in

God. The questions keep me on the exciting journey of discipleship and prepare me for the challenges that I face along the way. I know the journey is full of people who will love me, pray for me, and help me along the unknown paths ahead. I simply need to put my faith and trust in Jesus as Lord and depend on him to lead me far beyond what I could ever expect or imagine.

PETER CURTS (CHAPTER 3)

I remember feeling discontented and isolated when I was sixteen. I was unsure which peer group I best fit into. Did I belong with the honor roll students? My grades were good, but academics didn't drive me. Since my brother played sports, was I, too, destined to find my niche in athletics? I enjoyed sports but I had never been particularly competitive. Would I be most comfortable with the youth group at the church I attended? Some Christians struck me as socially awkward; besides, I often questioned if God existed.

One cold winter night I began to find my answers. I had a conversation over AOL Instant Messenger with a young woman I didn't know well. We engaged in a dialogue about what it means to have faith and live it out. Eventually I grew close to her family and saw how their faith was dynamic and always evolving. For them, a life with God gave them purpose every day. As my friendship continued to develop with this family, I discovered for myself that discipleship is a lifelong process that best unfolds in a community of believers. I wanted to be part of that community. That's where I belonged.

JENIFER STUELPE GIBBS (CHAPTER 4)

Even though it was nine o'clock in the evening, sweat dripped from our brows. After a hard day's work in southwestern Haiti, our mission team gathered on the porch to play dominoes and pray for a cool breeze. We had just met, so we used our evenings to get acquainted.

I looked forward to stories shared by the elderly couple. Adventures of loving and serving God stretched throughout the decades of their lives. Following Christ led them to take risks and make new friends all over the globe. Fervent prayers and memorized scripture verses served them as guideposts in unsure times. They ended every story with a bit of laughter and a nostalgic look saying, "Wow, did we see God at work that time!"

Until those evenings with that wise couple, I had not imagined following Christ as an ongoing story. I was new to faith at the time and thought it was something you did or didn't have. After those hot Haitian nights, I began to understand discipleship as a lifelong venture. I wondered about the stories I would be telling after walking with Christ for a few more decades.

BRIAN DURAND (CHAPTER 5)

I was confirmed while in sixth grade. I knew at the time that saying yes to following Jesus was important to my family. The occasion included gifts. I think I even knew it was important for me. I just didn't understand why. I had memorized the Apostles' Creed and learned all the seasons in the church calendar, but I didn't know what it meant to be a disciple of Jesus Christ.

Nearly ten years later, I had joined the church as an adult and felt woefully inadequate as I began volunteering in youth ministry. How could I mentor youth when I didn't feel like I knew anything about the Bible? A wise pastor and mentor suggested I enroll in DISCIPLE Bible Study. In the first few weeks of exploring the Bible with an amazing group, I realized what I had missed years earlier in confirmation class. Saying yes to following Jesus wasn't the end of a faith process but the beginning, a process I began when I said yes on confirmation Sunday. Thus, walking with youth as a strong faith mentor wasn't about having all the answers, but inviting them to follow Jesus Christ alongside me in the lifelong process of becoming disciples.

Brenda Freije (Chapter 6)

During my first year of law school, in Bloomington, Indiana, some classmates decided to take a break from studying and head to Bear's Place, a local hangout. They wanted to hear a new singer-songwriter in town and convinced me to join them for the concert. I was grateful for the time with friends, but only mildly interested in the music. My attitude changed the more I listened. With profound clarity, Carrie Newcomer sang about love and forgiveness, pain and redemption. I couldn't remember the last time I had been to church or had thought about these ideas. I suddenly realized how painfully distant I felt from God.

Proof that God reaches out to us wherever we are, I experienced a spiritual reawakening in a bar in Bloomington. A folk singer's lyrics pierced my heart and stirred a deep longing for God. I had stopped practicing my faith. I had strayed a long way from the discipleship path. Fortunately, even though we can get lost, God is always waiting to welcome us back. The journey home, I realized, would be a lifelong venture.

Kimberly King (Chapter 7)

My grandparents were my first example of people dedicated to spreading the good news of Jesus Christ. Their tireless work and devotion to the small faith community where I was baptized taught me the importance of making a commitment to spiritual growth.

I understood at an early age the significance of making a

personal commitment to serve Christ. After sitting through many altar calls, I made my commitment public at age eleven when I walked to the front of the church affirming my desire to be baptized.

I'm not sure of the moment when I realized that becoming a disciple of Jesus Christ is a lifelong venture, but reflecting on my journey convinces me that the process began at my small family church and continues to unfold daily. The years since my baptism have included many life transitions—marriage, motherhood, health crises, divorce, remarriage, a career change, surprise, disappointment, success, love, forgiveness, and grace. All my experiences confirm that God is always present. I experience God's presence in celebration and challenge. And with each transition I sense a deepening of my relationship with God, and I feel a profound knowing that God's love, forgiveness, and grace are always offered.

DAVID WILLIAMSON (CHAPTER 8)

The summer before my freshman year of high school, I asked Jesus into my heart. It wasn't a response to any altar call; I wasn't even at church. I was just lying in bed, reflecting on the testimony a senior had given at our youth group meeting earlier that night. There were no fireworks, no immediate confirmation that anything was different about me. I thought I'd messed up the prayer somehow.

During the next few months, I would respond to just about every altar call given, at church or at youth conferences, seeking confirmation that indeed Christ was in my life. Eventually someone explained that the Christian life didn't depend on emotions— whether I felt God was with me—but on God's promises, and so I stopped going forward to give my life to Jesus.

But here's what I didn't understand: I thought asking Jesus into my heart was a one-time event. However, I've found over the years that I have an incredible propensity to push Christ out of my heart, to allow other things to crowd my attention. And so, at various points throughout my walk as a Christian, I've felt the need to invite Jesus into my heart anew. Not because Christ is not already there, but because I need to reopen my heart again and again to his transforming presence.

I don't know that I'll ever outlive that need to open my heart to Jesus. I hope not to.

ADOLF HANSEN (CHAPTERS 9–11)

The Sunday evening service in the church in Brooklyn, New York, met in Fellowship Hall. Approximately 150 people were there. I was one of them—age fifteen.

Toward the end of the service the pastor asked if God was speaking to anyone about "full-time Christian service." I knew what that meant. I had heard it many times. But this particular night, I sensed that God might be speaking to me. And when the pastor asked if anyone was "willing" to go into such service, I thought that might be me. I wasn't ready to decide, but I was ready to be willing.

In response to the pastor's invitation, I found myself standing up. So did a couple of other youth, though not in the row where I was sitting. The atmosphere was quiet and contemplative— no music, and no emotional appeal. Just the gracious voice of a pastor inviting us to stand if we were "willing" to go into "full-time Christian service."

I did a lot of thinking after that service and talked with a lot of people. And in that process I began to realize that discipleship was going to be a lifelong process, whether I entered "full-time Christian service" or not.

A CLOSING WORD

If you are becoming a disciple of Jesus Christ, those of us who have written this chapter invite you to reflect on how you came to the realization that it is a lifelong process.

If you are not becoming a disciple of Jesus Christ, those of us who have written this chapter invite you to reflect on whether you want to begin the process.

Next Steps in the Venture

Becoming a disciple of Jesus Christ in the twenty-first century

You've read about steps the writers of this book have taken during their ventures of becoming disciples of Jesus Christ. You've also read about steps others have taken. Now it's your turn to review the steps you've taken, to reflect on those steps, and to formulate what your next steps will be.

As you review the steps you've taken on your personal venture, bring to mind the points set forth in chapters 9 and 10, and then carry out the following:

1. In your life

- Trace the path you've followed in your experience of becoming a disciple of Jesus Christ—where you began, where you moved next, and so on.
- Invite one or more persons to trace the path they've followed in becoming a disciple of Jesus Christ and—if they're willing—to share that path with you, as you share your path with them.

2. In your congregation (particularly if you're a pastor or a layperson in a leadership position)

- Organize a new group, or use an existing group (perhaps a new member class), to read and discuss this book in a format that corresponds with your situation.
- Have persons in the group trace their paths (as suggested above) and then share with one another.

As you, either personally or with a group in your congregation, reflect on the steps already taken, try to recall the variables identified in chapters 11 and 12, and then share what you and others have learned about discipleship, including ways persons have become, are becoming, and may become disciples of Jesus Christ.

If you are musically inclined, look over the refrain on the following page, and then play it on a musical instrument and/or sing it. If, on the other hand, you are not so inclined, find a friend who might carry out such possibilities with you. And if you have an individual or group in your congregation who might play or sing it, share a copy with them.

Finally, if it seems fitting in your life, and/or the life of one or more groups in your congregation, formulate a plan for next steps. And then—if this is your way—write out your overall plan in such a manner that you identify specific steps and correlate them with specific dates for their accomplishment. If this is not your way, carry out your overall plan in whatever manner makes most sense to you.

It's not important how you take your next steps! It's important that you take them!

Make Disciples of Jesus

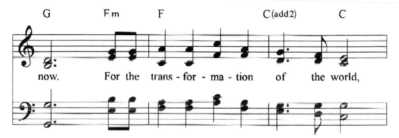

Words: The United Methodist Church Mission, adapt. Adolf Hansen
Music: Folk melody, arr. Adolf Hansen and Brenda Freije
© 2013 Adolf Hansen

Afterword

I have been privileged to travel and work across the vast global connection of The United Methodist Church. These opportunities have emerged through a number of mission partnerships initiated by the West Ohio, Minnesota, and Dakotas annual conferences, my presidencies of the General Board of Global Ministries and the Connectional Table, my assignment to provide episcopal oversight of the United Methodist Missions in Vietnam, Laos, and Thailand, and my membership on the denomination's Standing Committee on Central Conference Matters.

Throughout the United Methodist connection I sense a growing awareness of and commitment to our mission to make disciples of Jesus Christ for the transformation of the world. There is also a deepening affirmation that disciple-making primarily occurs in local churches. I will never forget the Sunday morning I was worshiping in a United Methodist congregation in Kinshasa, Democratic Republic of Congo, and the pastor began the service by declaring, "The mission of our congregation is to make disciples of Christ for the transformation of the world." The number of vital, missional congregations is growing. New congregations are forming. Established congregations are bearing the kingdom fruits of growing in love of God and neighbor, reaching new, younger, and more diverse people, and healing a broken world.

Yet, the most frequent questions that people ask me throughout my travels are: Just what is a Christian disciple? What does a disciple of Jesus Christ look like? Act like? Become? These questions reveal a more fundamental concern that I have observed throughout The United Methodist Church and many other faith traditions. Many congregations do not have a defined process for making or forming disciples. Without clarity on what constitutes a Christian disciple, designing such a process is difficult, perhaps impossible. It is one thing to have a common understanding and expression of our mission; it is quite another thing to understand how one becomes a disciple and to develop the processes for forming devoted, mature disciples of Jesus.

The Indiana Conference's experience, reflected in *Becoming a Disciple*, affirms this central truth and offers a practical, comprehensive paradigm for helping persons and congregations grow in discipleship. The chapters illustrate in warm and personal ways that the vitality of the global United Methodist witness is contingent upon keeping our stated mission the main thing, unencumbered by worthy, but often extraneous, projects and agendas; clarifying what constitutes a disciple of Jesus; affirming the local church as the most significant arena for disciple-making; and aligning our resources to support the development of fruitful disciple-making processes in our congregations.

The bottom line—clearly articulated in *Becoming a Disciple*—is that disciples of Jesus glorify God in all they do, with all they are, and in all they are becoming. Disciples of Jesus live only for God. Disciples of Jesus order their lives according to Christ's teachings. Disciples of Jesus are Spirit-filled and Spirit-fruitful. Disciples of Jesus value life together. Disciples of Jesus serve others. Disciples of Jesus carry Christ into a broken, hurting world. Disciples of Jesus have heart-eyes to see God's presence in this life and in the life to come. Disciples of Jesus are evangels of the good news. All to the glory of God, forever and ever.

Everywhere I travel, I encounter United Methodists and Christians from other traditions, hungry to live as authentic, devoted disciples of Jesus and to participate more fully in God's mission of transforming the world and ushering in the fullness of God's reign. I am grateful to the Indiana Conference for offering a pathway that speaks to this universal hunger—a pathway that is essential to the work of the Connectional Table and the Council of Bishops in promoting an increase in the number of vital congregations.

Bruce R. Ough
Bishop, Dakotas-Minnesota Area
The United Methodist Church

About the Authors

Peter Curts is the Teaching Pastor at Wesley Chapel UMC, in Floyds Knobs, Indiana. Together with members of his congregation, he is engaged in numerous projects in the community, particularly mentoring and tutoring in various local schools. Peter also traveled with Operation Classroom to Sierra Leone, West Africa.

Brian Durand is the Lead Pastor at Clay UMC in South Bend, Indiana. Prior to coming to his present position, he served as the Indiana Conference Associate Director of Leadership Development. Brian was also an adjunct faculty member in the Department of Philosophy and Religion at the University of Indianapolis.

Brenda Freije is the Director of Networking and Recruitment and General Counsel for the Christian Theological Seminary in Indianapolis. She earned the doctor of jurisprudence degree from the Indiana University Mauer School of Law and practiced law before enrolling in seminary. Brenda teaches in the area of worship arts and design and frequently leads worship as a vocalist.

Jenifer Stuelpe Gibbs is the Pastor of Connection at Meridian Street UMC in Indianapolis. Prior to attending seminary she worked as an educational professional development coach at the Indiana Department of Education. Jen also traveled to South Africa as a participant in the Wabash Pastoral Leadership Program (funded by Lilly Endowment).

Jill Moffett Howard is the Pastor at Morgantown UMC in Morgantown, Indiana. One of her travels was with Eva Mozes Kor, a Holocaust survivor, to the Auschwitz concentration camp in Poland. Jill is also a musical vocalist, performing in community theater as well as in church settings.

Kimberly King is the Pastor of Congregational Care at

St. Luke's UMC in Indianapolis. She earned the master of arts in marriage and family therapy as well as her divinity degree. Prior to attending seminary she was employed in a corporate setting.

David Williamson is the Pastor of Family and Worship Ministries at St. Luke's UMC in Indianapolis. Following graduation from seminary, he and his wife spent two years in ministry in Haiti, becoming fluent in the Creole language. Dave continues to lead groups—youth as well as adults—to serve in a variety of ministries in that country.

Brent Wright is the Pastor at Broad Ripple UMC in Indianapolis. Prior to attending seminary, he earned a master's in education degree and taught middle school science. Brent also traveled to South Africa as a participant in the Wabash Pastoral Leadership Program (funded by Lilly Endowment).

Adolf Hansen is the Theologian in Residence at St. Luke's UMC in Indianapolis. He is also Senior Scholar and Vice President Emeritus at Garrett-Evangelical Theological Seminary in Evanston, Illinois. Earlier in his career, Adolf was a professor and department chair at the University of Indianapolis.

CPSIA information can be obtained at www.ICGtesting.com
Printed in the USA
LVOW10s0036260315

432008LV00003B/5/P